– *50* –
HILL WALKS
in
THE CHILTERNS

Don Hinson

Published by Sigma Leisure – an imprint of
Sigma Press, 1 South Oak Lane, Wilmslow, Cheshire SK9 6AR, England.

British Library Cataloguing in Publication Data
A CIP record for this book is available from the British Library.

ISBN: 1-85058-662-4

Typesetting and Design by: Sigma Press, Wilmslow, Cheshire.

Cover photograph: Looking east to Fingest and the hills beyond

Maps and photographs: the author

Printed by: MFP Design and Print

Disclaimer: the information in this book is given in good faith and is believed to be correct at the time of publication. No responsibility is accepted by either the author or publisher for errors or omissions, or for any loss or injury howsoever caused. Only you can judge your own fitness, competence and experience.

Preface

The Saxon word 'chilt' means 'chalk', and it is the chalk that helps to make the Chilterns an officially designated area of outstanding natural beauty (AONB). There is something for everyone to enjoy: the wonderful views and the carpet of flowers, from fragrant thyme to exotic orchids, on the chalk downs; the glorious beech woods - majestic without leaves in winter, brilliant green when fresh in spring, or best of all in autumn tints which must be seen to be believed; the unspoilt rural villages, many with churches and buildings of special interest; the pattern of fields reflecting the dominance of agriculture, with little industrialisation.

When you add to all this a network of 1500 miles of public paths, mostly well-kept, you have a wonderful opportunity of exploring this beautiful countryside on foot. In this book there are 50 circular walks of up to 9 miles. Many of these can be shortened, so there are over 50 in the 3 to 5 mile range. They provide a comprehensive coverage of the scenic regions of the area, and avoid as far as possible the less pleasant paths (e.g. long stretches of muddy bridleways). The area of the Chilterns is hard to define. For walking purposes it might be taken as the area between the escarpment and the Rivers Thames, Colne and Ver. To help you navigate your way, the instructions are clear and concise. They are nearly always beside the map (not on another page) and are numbered so you can easily relate them to the map in the book or to an Ordnance Survey map. I hope you will enjoy using them.

Don Hinson

Contents

Index to information panels

Before You Begin

How to Follow a Route

As well as this book, it is worth taking a map with you. Two superb maps, the Ordnance Survey Explorer 2 and 3 (Chiltern Hills: North and South), cover the walks (except numbers 45, 49, 50 and part of 37) at the large scale of 1:25 000 ($2\frac{1}{2}$ inches to a mile or 4cm to 1km). Or, at half this scale, there are O.S. Pathfinder 165 (Aylesbury and Leighton Buzzard), 166 (Luton and Hertford) and 175 (Reading and Windsor). It is useful to mark the route on the map in pencil.

The written descriptions of the routes are brief, but, I hope, clear. Before using this book, browse through the glossary and abbreviations to get a general idea of the terms used. Note that 'up' and 'down' always refer to gradients. (Unlike everyday speech where you may go 'up' a level road to post a letter.)

A walk can be started at any convenient point along the route. A grid reference is given for the suggested start. The first three numbers refer to the grid lines which indicate how far east the point is; the last three to how far north. Thus, in the first walk, 683 means the start is three tenths of the way between the vertical lines marked 68 and 69, and 903 means it is three tenths of the way between the horizontal lines marked 90 and 91.

In deteriorating weather or shortage of time it may be possible to make a short cut by roads, and these are shown on the maps of this book. Rarely, a path is obstructed e.g. by overgrowth, mud, or being ploughed up. You are entitled to remove an obstruction as far as necessary for you to get by, or to get round it by a short detour. If crops cover a right of way, you may walk through them, and with care will do little damage.

Glossary

down: the path descends

drive: track leading to private house or farm (usually surfaced)

farm gate: gate wide enough for vehicles to get through

lane: small, surfaced public road

on: keep walking in about the same direction

path: a way too narrow for vehicles

pole: wooden device for carrying telephone or electricity cables etc.

thicket: mini-wood consisting of shrubs or small trees

track: a way big enough for vehicles (could be grassy, stony, concrete or even muddy)

up: the path rises

Abbreviations

⮡: is a reminder that a shorter walk follows a different route at this point

alt: marks an alternative route on the map

E: east

km: kilometre = 0.625 miles

L: turn left through about 90 degrees. Note, however, that 'fork L' means take the left hand of two paths at a fork. This will not involve turning 90 degrees – sometimes you may not turn at all.

½L: turn left through about 45 degrees

⅓L: turn left through about 30 degrees

⅔L: turn left through about 60 degrees

loo: indicates location of public toilets on map

m: metre. This is about a yard. All distances are approximate.

N: north

P: parking

R: turn right through about 90 degrees

S: south

W: west

Maps

The maps in this book are based on the first edition of the Explorer Maps 2 and 3 (Chiltern Hills), with a few walks on the adjacent sheets, with the sanction of the Controller of Her Majesty's Stationery Office.

To the best of my knowledge, all paths used are public ones. Most Chiltern paths are in a reasonable condition; many are marked by white or yellow arrows. I hope my maps are reasonably accurate, but any paths and features not on O.S. maps, may only be shown approximately.

In choosing a route, I have aimed at using paths with good views wherever possible. I have tried to avoid roads, muddy bridleways, paths which are difficult to follow, and those which do not offer much variety e.g. those which stay in woods a long time. My wife has made useful comments on the various routes we followed, and I am grateful also for the typing she has done.

Things to See on the Way

Interesting churches, manors and houses are often close to these walks, so brief details are given. Wild flowers are a delight, especially on the chalk downland and in some woods (before the trees are in leaf). The Warburg nature reserve (walk 9) is outstanding in this respect, with a fine show of orchids. Apart from the usual birds, watch out for the magnificent red kites, now often seen effortlessly gliding the skies, on any of the walks from 1 to 22. If you are interested in food for free, blackberries are the only reliable harvest. Edible fungi can be found, but should not be eaten unless properly identified.

If you wish to eat out, there is often an inn or two shown on the map. Use the Yellow Pages to phone and check what they offer. Cafés and tearooms are seldom found, except in the small towns on or near the route.

Transport

Cars can be parked off the road, or in a quiet side road where the letter 'P' appears on the map. Parking is free unless otherwise stated.

A rough guide to public transport is given below. You should check details by phoning the enquiry service 0345 382000 (Bucks), 0345 244344 (Herts) or using their website:
http://www.pindar.co.uk/bucks/
before setting out. Numbers in brackets refer to walks within 400m of a bus stop or station. 'Frequent' means about a 30-minute service or better. 'Infrequent' means over 2 hours.

Trains run frequently from London to Amersham, Great Missenden (32), Wendover (800m to walk 42) and Chesham (38) – Metropolitan line.

From Marylebone to High Wycombe (for buses) there is a roughly 1 hour service.

From Euston to Watford (for buses), Berkhamstead (for buses) and Tring (frequent) (800m to walk 47).

Buses from High Wycombe to:

Speen (22, 23 and 25) infrequent – none Sat., Sun.

Princes Risborough (22, 23, 24 and 28) frequent – 2 hour Sun.

Stokenchurch (16 and 19 – 22) frequent – 1 hour Sat., 2 hour Sun.

Radnage (17) 2 hour – infrequent Sat., none Sun.

Ibstone (4) 2 hour – none Sat., Sun.

Bledlow Ridge (17 – 22) 2 hour – none Sun.

Bradenham (18 – 22) 2 hour – none Sun.

Downley (22) frequent – none Sun.

Great Missenden (22 and 32) 1 hour – none Sun.

Loudwater (34) 1 hour

Henley (10, 11 and 12) frequent – 2 hour Sun.

Chesham (35, 38 and 41) frequent – 2 hour Sun.

From Henley to:

Watlington (2, 3, 7, 8 and 11) infrequent – none Sun.

From Hemel Hempstead to:

Aldbury, Tring (45 and 46) infrequent – not Sun.

Whipsnade (50) 2 hour – not Sun.

Chesham (38) 1 hour – not Sun.

Potten End, Tring (43 and 45) frequent – 2 hour Sun.

From Dunstable to:

Ivinghoe, Tring (43 and 48) 2 hour

From Chesham to:

Watford (35, 38, 40 and 41) 1 hour – not Sun.

Leyhill (37 and 38) 1 hour – not Sat, Sun.

From Amersham to:

Berkhamstead (35, 38, 41 and 44) 1 hour – not Sun.

Beaconsfield (35) 2 hour – not Sun.

Things to Take on your Walk

* Rucksack containing food, drink, first aid kit and compass.

* Clothes for wet or cold weather, walking shoes and sunglasses. Don't forget keys, money, maps, this book, membership cards and identification books.

* A camera and binoculars can add to your enjoyment of the walks.

* Finally, knowing the weather forecast could be useful – do you need extra layers or a sunscreen?

Location maps for walks

Dashed lines show the main walks.
Solid lines are where two walks use the same route.
Dotted lines show short cuts.
Numbers refer to the walks in this book.

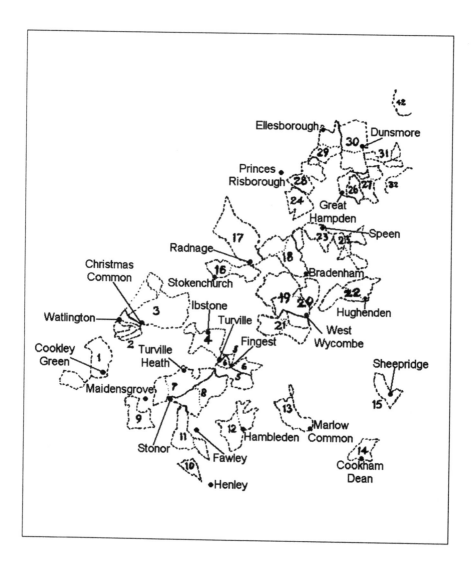

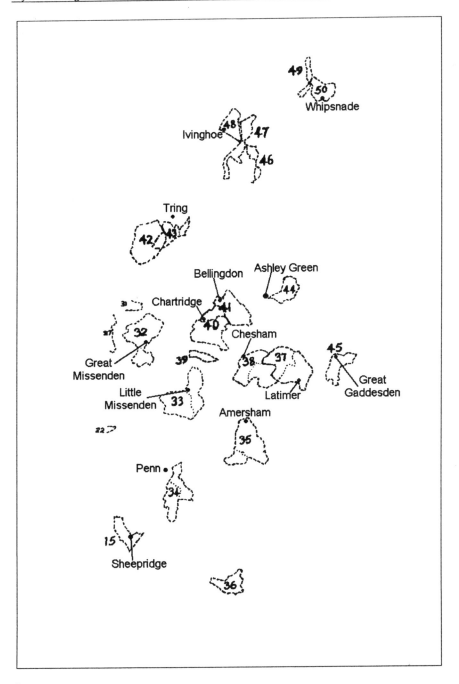

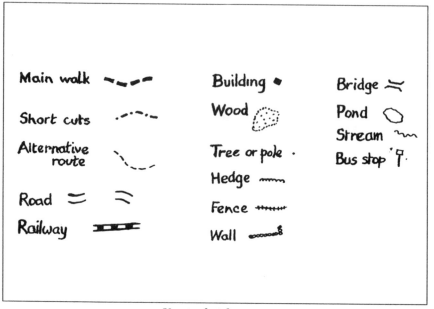

Key to sketch maps

1. Ewelme and Swyncombe Downs

Starting Point: Swyncombe Church (683 903).

Access: At Cookley Green. 6 miles (10km) NW of Henley, turn W off the B481 and at once go L at a junction. After 1300m (1km) turn L and park near the church.

Distance: 9 miles (14km). It can easily be shortened.

Detail: The downs make good walking with wide views and attractive beech woods. You climb nearly 1000ft.

Map: Explorer 3 (W) or Pathfinder 175.

At Swyncombe, there is a manor house and a church which was partly built in the 11th century. Items of interest inside include a 14th-century bell. Outside you will find a carpet of snowdrops and winter aconite in February. Driving a few miles W will bring you to Ewelme, and an attractive church with almshouses beside it.

Near Swyncombe

1. Walk back (N) to the road turning and go on down track.

2. On into wood. Stay on the main path.

3. Track bears L to farm.

4. Just after farm go $\frac{1}{2}$R for 40m then R again.

5. On over road.

6. At junction of five tracks just past house, go sharp R along surfaced drive.

7. On along track where drive turns R.

8. On in wood, mostly on bank just L of track. Soon fork R up.

9. Over road and $\frac{1}{2}$R along lane.

10. Sharp R along road.

11. Ignore track at wood edge, but 50m on go $\frac{1}{2}$L over stile. Later ignore crossing track.

12. Go $\frac{1}{3}$R over field to small, iron gate 30m L of pole.

13. On over drive. R into churchyard, passing L of church.

14. Turn L down bridleway, soon bearing $\frac{1}{2}$L.

15. At signpost go L up field into wood. On up and out of wood.

16. On along field edge. Bear $\frac{1}{2}$R along edge to field corner.

17. Here on along track.

18. Pass barn on your L, then turn L for 100m to cross-track.

19. Here R down track.

20. Where stony track ends keep on along L edge of field. (Ignore track along R edge.)

21. On in next fields (fence on your R at first).

22. Turn R up track.

23. Turn R along drive beside line of trees.

24. Go $\frac{1}{2}$L along small bridleway in wood (50m before drive bears R). On leaving wood go on along field edge (hedge on your L). Soon bear R with hedge.

25. On in wood.

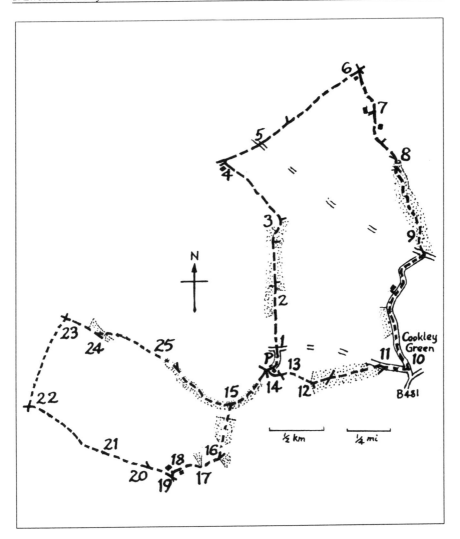

Variations

Swincombe Downs (5 miles, 8km, 600ft): Simply follow 1 to 13.

Ewelme Downs (4 miles, 6km, 400ft): Walk past the church (on your L) and go ½L down bridleway. Follow 15 to 25.

2. Watlington Hill

Starting Point: Watlington Hill car park (710 936).

Access: From Watlington, go SE, uphill, for 1 mile or so.

Distance: 8 miles (12.5km) and easily shortened.

Detail: A fine introduction to this chalky hill, which is seen from many angles. You climb 1100ft.

Map: Explorer 3 (W) or Pathfinder 175.

From the top of the hill you go down to the Ridgeway for an optional tour of the escarpment NE of the hill. A new path then takes you to a pleasant valley climb and a lovely wood from which you emerge to enjoy more views during the final down and upon your return. The shorter walk avoids slightly tricky route finding at stage 5 and possible mud at stages 7 and 9. Other obvious short cuts can be seen on the map. The large chalk mark (at 700 939) was cut in 1764. The town has a 14th-century church and many interesting 16th-century buildings.

1. Go towards Watlington over grass, then by path beside road.
2. Go ½L to open hill. On along wide grass strip just below ridge top, gently bearing R.
3. Down ridge, aiming just R of Watlington. Fork R just after large, white chalk mark. ↘
4. Down road and R along Ridgeway track.
5. Go ⅓R along path at stile. (If overgrown here, try an unofficial path 100m further along track.) It gently climbs, reaching a more open area. Here stay by shrubs on your R. (Ignore a L fork.)
6. There is a fence on your R for a while. On in trees to stile.
7. Down field to bottom corner. Over stile and down path.
8. On past buildings.
9. L along track.
10. On over road, soon fork R.
11. At gate go ½L over field to bottom of wood, where a path is joined.
12. Go down to gate and R along path.

13. After house go sharp L along track. Soon ignore L fork.

14. At junction go ½L to pass L of buildings. On along grass track.

15. R along road; R at both junctions.

16. Turn ½R along drive opposite church.

17. After 100m go ½R along path. Follow arrows. Later fork R down.

18. Near wood edge bear L along edge, staying inside wood.

19. On over clearing into wood for 10m, then R down field.

20. On along track and sharp R along path after house on R.

21. Soon after passing steps ignore path forking R. Gently climb by wood edge.

22. At open area go L up to open skyline. On down until just clear of shrubs. Then R along level grass, curving L to a clear path. Back the way you came.

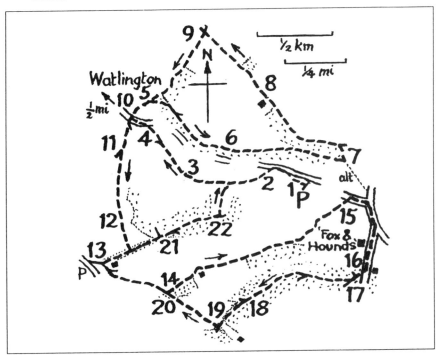

Variation

Shorter walk (5½ miles, 9km, 600ft): Follow 1 to 3. Then down road, L along track, soon fork R and follow 11 to 22.

3. Shirburn

Starting Point: Cowleaze Wood car park (725 955).

Access: From Watlington, drive SE to Christmas Common. Here turn sharp L 1½ miles (2.5km) to the parking.

Distance: 9 miles (14km) or much less.

Detail: A tour of the Chiltern escarpment and its adjoining woods and valleys. You climb 1300ft.

Map: Explorer 3 (W) or Pathfinder 165 and 175.

The scarp is first visited, then there's a long, gentle, wooded descent to reach a pleasant valley path. After a ridge climb and drop to a farm, there are splendid views as you return to Cowleaze Wood. As a final challenge, you can tackle the scarp again and walk the Icknield Way, one of Britain's oldest roads – probably 4000 years old. The bridleway (stage 7) is sometimes muddy. Cowleaze Wood has a number of sculptures within it and waymarked walks.

1. Take path SW, parallel to road, then along road by water tower and ½R over field to far corner.
2. Over stile and down track, soon in the open.
3. Path later goes between wood and fence. Then it leaves fence and you soon bear R along track.
4. Bear R along path to wood edge and go L beside fence.
5. Path crosses track. Soon it joins track. ↝
6. Go L along lane.
7. On up track, then path. (Wood by your R, later also L.)
8. Near top cross stile on R and go ½R up field. On by hedge on your R to road.
9. L along road 100m and R along track, passing just R of tower.
10. Fork ⅓L along path. Follow arrows. Go ½R where path comes in on L, thus nearing wood edge.

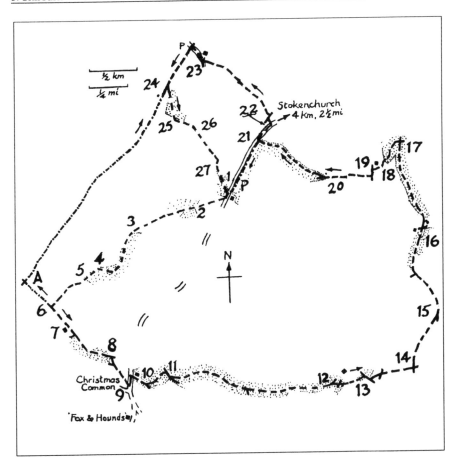

11. Here take L fork gently down in wood.

12. 100m before buildings, go R following arrows. Soon you cross a track and follow path by wood edge (on your R).

13. R for 30m along track and ½L up field to stile. Here on over track and down field to hedge gap.

14. Through and L along track.

15. On along drive.

16. Ignore L fork to buildings. 100m later go ½L up track. It bears L as it passes house on R.

17. Go L down crossing path.

18. Leaving wood go ½L down field, passing L of farm. Over stile and up to next stile.

19. L along drive 60m and R up field.

20. Into wood 30m L of pole. Fork R along wood edge. ↘

21. Turn R along road.

22. Turn L at white arrow and R along old road. Soon L down track.

23. On past farm, then L along track (by poles).

24. 100m before double pole, go ½L through gap to stile and on in wood.

25. Leave wood and go ½L along its edge. On to double pole.

26. Go ½R beside fence on your L. On over stile.

27. Over next stile, R 5m and L up track.

Variations

Shorter walk (7 miles, 11km, 1000ft): Follow 1 to 20. Then go L along path beside road.

Much shorter walk (4 miles, 6.5km, 400ft): Follow 1 to 5. Then go R along lane.

A. Turn R at cross track.

24. 100m past double pole go sharp R through gap to stile and on in wood. Follow 25 to 27.

4. Turville to Ibstone

Starting Point: The car park between the inn and church in Turville (768 911).

Access: Use minor roads e.g. from Lane End on the B482.

Distance: 8½ miles (13.5km). Can be shortened.

Detail: A switchback route of views, a windmill, ridges and woods met between two villages. You climb 1650ft.

Map: Explorer 3 (W) or Pathfinder 175.

There has been a windmill here since 1293. The present 17th-century smock-mill, now converted into a house, looks down on the delightful village of Turville and its medieval church. There is also a Norman church at stage 33 which is worth a visit. There may be a few muddy patches e.g. at 13 and 15.

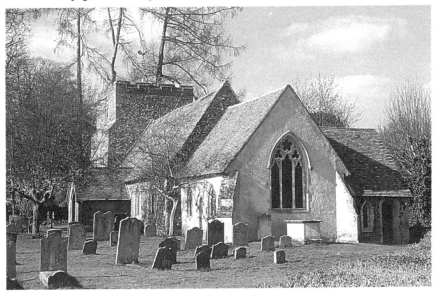

Turville church

1. Take footpath opposite phone box. On up with fence on your R.
2. At road go R, soon L down track in wood.
3. After 100m go over stile on L and down path.
4. Down to field corner.
5. Go over stile, on 10m and sharp L along valley.
6. Soon after narrow wood, go R up track between fences. On up drive, then lane.
7. At stile (60m before road junction) go sharp L over field. On over next fields. On beside hedge.
8. At wood go R 50m, L over stile and down wood.
9. At bottom, turn L along the R of two gently diverging tracks. After 100m fork R up track.
10. On up field with hedge on your R. Later a young wood on your L.
11. L along road. R over stile along enclosed path. On over field.
12. At bottom go up path. Later bear R to drive. ⬎
13. Here turn R. Just after Ibstone Cottage, go L up stony track. After Farside Cottage bear R along grass track.
14. Soon cross stony track and go ½R along field edge (wide hedge on your L).
15. When path bends R, go ½L and very soon L along track in wood.
16. Watch for path junction. Go ½L down path and out of wood.
17. R along field edge to valley bottom.
18. L along track (hedge on your R).
19. At wide, stony track go sharp L over field to stile into wood.
20. Bear R along path. Soon ½L down track.
21. On over field into wood. On up path, soon winding up steep hill.
22. It bears L 20m before top wood edge. Soon R on path to field.
23. On over field, then between fences. On along drive to lane.
24. R along lane.
25. Later go down track just L of lane. Rejoin lane later.
26. Turn L with lane to gate and R down track.
27. Where track bends ½L, go on over stile and down field to trees.
28. On in trees, over track, on up field to lane.
29. L down lane. Near gate on L, go ½L along track to junction.
30. Here ½R along track. Soon fork L up path. On over drive.
31. Bear L to stile and uphill (fence on your R). Keep along wood edge (on your R) to stile by trough.
32. Go R up in wood. On over track.

33. At top go into churchyard, past church (on your L) to lane.

34. Here turn L. On reaching road go R down it.

35. Where it bends R, go on along level path.

36. After slight descent, track bends L towards top of wood. Here go R down to fence. Keep along fence, between wood edge and fence.

37. Over stile and down field to stile. Over and down path into wood.

38. Out of wood down to stiles. Over and down path to houses. L along road.

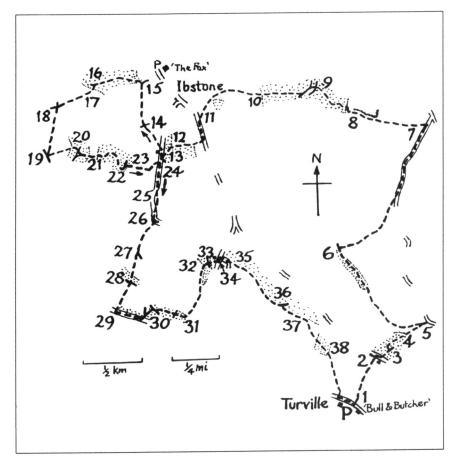

Variation

Shorter walk (7 miles, 11km, 1300ft): Follow 1 to 12. Go L along lane and follow 25 to 38.

5. Around Fingest

Starting Point: The car park between inn and church in Turville (768 911).

Access: Use minor roads e.g. from Lane End on the B482.

Distance: 6 miles (9.5km). Can be shortened.

Detail: A walk with many fine views, a windmill, beech woods and two attractive villages. You climb 1000ft.

Map: Explorer 3 (W) or Pathfinder 175.

Fingest church has a Norman tower with an unusual, twin-gabled roof. For details of Turville see walk 4. Paths are good, but there can be a few muddy patches e.g. around stage 2.

1. Go SW along the lane that starts by the car park. On along path.
2. On across field for 150m. Then ½L to gate at L corner of wood.
3. Through gate and along track past pipeline. On over field to wood.
4. Up in wood and L along main track.
5. Where track ends, follow path R along wood edge (soon between fences), then L to drive and road.
6. R along road. L just before pub.
7. Into field and ½R along field edge near line of poles.
8. L at road. Soon R up track.
9. At wood fork L.
10. Up field with bank on your L. On over lane.
11. L along road. Keep on when road turns R.
12. Stay on track as it turns L along wood edge. Keep on as it enters wood.
13. At wide gate on wood edge, go on over field into wood.
14. Out of wood and down by its edge.
15. At wood bottom go ½R to road. L along road. ↳ R at junction.
16. Go R up path 50m after church. Over stile and ½L up fields.

17. On up wood. Ignore side turnings.

18. After slight descent, go L along path. Soon ½L down at junction.

19. Fork R down to wood edge and on to road.

20. R along road. Soon ½L over stile and up field. Up path in wood.

21. Over stile and up track to road. R along road.

22. Soon L down by fence or hedge on your L. On to start.

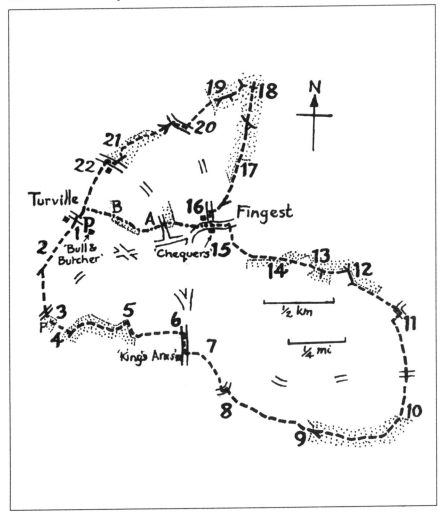

Variation

Shorter walk (4½ miles, 7km, 500ft): Follow 1 to 14 and 15 up to ↘.
50m after church go on along path and ½L at path junction.

A. On over road, soon with a line of beeches on your L.

B. On down field, then L to road.

The windmill above Turville

6. A Fingest Figure of Eight

Starting Point: Fingest, near church and pub (777 912).

Access: Use minor roads e.g. from Lane End on the B482.

Distance: 5½ miles (8.5km). Can be shortened.

Detail: A second chance to enjoy this lovely area. You climb 750ft.

Map: Explorer 3 (W) or Pathfinder 175.

The flowers near stage 4 are quite special e.g. orchids and the rare Dragon's Teeth. Manor Farm, just N of Fingest, has some fine flint barns. By ending the walk after stage 15 it becomes a 4-mile (6km) walk and 500ft climb.

Looking down on Turville

1. Go N along lane away from the pub, and R up path 50m beyond the church. Over stile and on along field edge.

2. On up track. Later fork R, still along field edges.

3. Before long hill up, go R 50m to lane and R along it.

4. When lane turns R, go L over stile. Follow hedges on your R.

5. After a slight descent go L at field corner. On in wood.

6. On out of wood and along field edge. At corners go R and R again, keeping fence on your L.

7. On by wood on your R. When wood bears R, keep on to hidden stile and lane.

8. Up steps and field, bearing gently away from fence, to stile. Here go $\frac{1}{2}$R up path in wood.

9. Keep on over crossing path.

10. L at next crossing path. On between fences.

11. R along track.

12. Stay on track as it turns L along wood edge. Keep on it as it enters wood.

13. At wide gate on wood edge, go on over field into wood.

14. Out of wood and down by its edge.

15. At wood bottom go $\frac{1}{2}$R to road. L along road. ➴

16. 50m after church go on along path (wall on your L). Go $\frac{1}{2}$L at path junction.

17. On over road, soon by line of beeches on your L.

18. On down field to corner, then R uphill with fence on your R.

19. At road go R, soon L down track in wood.

20. After 100m go over stile on L and down path.

21. Down to field corner and R along lane.

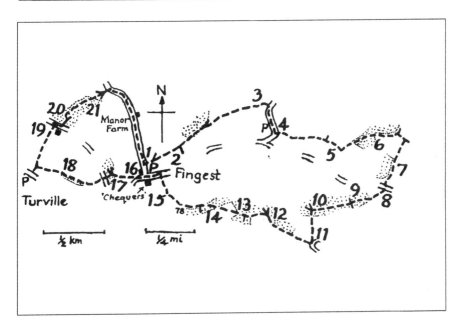

Water in the Chilterns

Much of the rain soaks through the chalk to reach an impervious layer such as clay. There it forms underground lakes, which emerge as springs at the foot of the hills, e.g. the source of the River Wye just west of West Wycombe (walks 19 – 21). Others include the River Chess near Chesham (37 and 38), the Misbourne near Great Missenden (32 and 33) and the Gade near Great Gaddesden (45). However, where clay with flints overlays the chalk there can be a few ponds and streams. Watercress grows wild, and has also been cultivated near Chesham and at other places.

Water supplies caused problems in parts of the Chilterns. At Turville Park (740 911), a 350-feet well in solid chalk was found to have the date 1308 scratched near the bottom. The Maharajah's Well in Stoke Row (679 841) reached water at a depth of 365ft. This ornate edifice was given by the Maharajah of Benares in 1863 in gratitude for the work done in India by Edward Reade, who had mentioned his village's water problem.

There is no sea water in the Chilterns, but there is part of a ship near walk 32. When Britain's last wooden battleship, the *Howe*, built in 1860, was scrapped, the huge figurehead, an oak bust of Admiral Howe weighing two tonnes, was moved to a garden near The Lee, where it can be seen from the lane at 490 039.

7. From Stonor to near Turville

Starting Point: Lay-by on the B480 at Stonor, 200m N of the T-junction, near footpath sign.

Access: Drive 4½ miles (7km) N from Henley along the A4130, then fork R along the B480.

Distance: 8 miles (12.5km). Can be shortened.

Detail: You see a deer park, a mansion and a series of delightful views, and climb 1150ft.

Map: Explorer 3 (W) or Pathfinder 175.

Near Stonor

The name Stonor probably refers to two 4000-year-old stone circles which survived until an 11th-century chapel was built. A stone circle was re-erected near the house in 1980. The interesting house and grounds are open on certain days. (Phone 01491 638 587) Mistletoe can be seen in trees near the house. In the deer park, please keep to the footpath, with **all** dogs on leads. If you see a fawn don't touch it or it will be deserted by the doe.

The Chilterns in the Twentieth Century

The Metropolitan railway line gave rise (with the help of advertisement) to many areas of new housing in the Chilterns from which commuting to work in London was convenient. The region became known as 'Metroland'. Examples of these include Gerrards Cross, formerly a small village, and Amersham on the Hill, above the unspoilt Old Amersham. Away from these areas the land is still quite thinly populated. Walkers from London were also encouraged to explore the area with the help of London Transport's books of walks that could be reached by train or bus.

New roads are fortunately few in this hilly area, the M40 being the most evident, slicing right through the escarpment. Recent bypasses at Tring, Amersham and Wendover have slightly affected walks from these towns.

Changes in farming have not had a major impact. The majority of old hedges still remain. Lack of grazing has led to an invasion of scrub and trees on the downs and commons. (Coombe Hill, though still open on top, looks very different now from its almost treeless appearance in the early part of the 20th century.) Brilliant yellow fields of oilseed rape are now common, and sometimes the delicate blue haze of flax is found. The few rivers in the area have often dried out recently, and this is a matter of great concern. Yet despite the changes (telephone and power cables are everywhere and hard to keep out of photographs) the basic unique character of the area is still there for you to enjoy. The Chiltern Society (113 Vale Road, Chesham, HP5 3HP) has made a valuable contribution to maintaining the footpaths and seeing that the attractive features of the area are not spoilt.

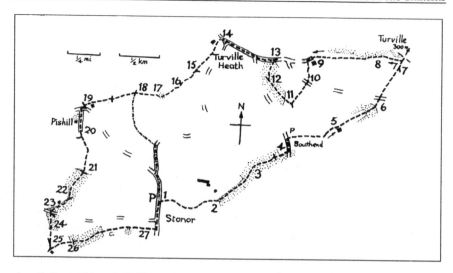

1. Follow clear path E, at right angles to road.
2. After passing Stonor House, the path runs just inside a thinly wooded area. Ignore crossing paths.
3. On where path joins track.
4. L along road for 150m, then R along track.
5. At farm go on down ridge (at first with fence on your R).
6. At road, on over field.
7. 40m before reaching hedge, turn sharp L up path past the L-hand of poles.
8. On up ridge, near wood on your R.
9. On along lane 50m then L down field (hedge on your L).
10. Over lane. On up field, soon in small valley. Later bear R to stile into wood.
11. On along path (white arrows).
12. Fork R to follow wider track.
13. Go L along lane. Keep on at junctions.
14. Go L along drive marked 'Saviors'. On along path just L of gate. Pass house and go on over field to stile. On over stiles to gate.
15. Through kissing gate and ½R by fence on your R.
16. On down fields.

17. At trees go down open field to crossing track. ⮧

18. Up field on top of bank, over lane and down field (hedge on your L).

19. After passing barn, go L along track to road. Here go R 50m and L along smaller road.

20. Go ⅓L along track. Go on (hedge on your L) at path junction.

21. On up in wood.

22. At top, keep on inside wood, near its edge (on your R) to road.

23. Over road and straight up path near R edge of wood.

24. At top corner, on over field towards buildings.

25. At field edge, turn sharpish L over field to white arrows on tree. Make for stile at wood edge.

26. On down wooded, then open ridge to road.

27. Here L along road and past T-junction.

Variations

Shorter walk (6 miles, 10km, 800ft): Follow 1 to 17, then L along crossing track, R along road and past T-junction.

The Medieval Chilterns

William the Conqueror made many organisational changes to society, but signs of these are not seen in the landscape. However, many buildings have survived – especially the flint churches. Few castles remain, except ruins at Berkhamstead and the complete, brick Shirburn Castle. Bricks were made at Nettlebed right up to the 20th century and the kiln can still be seen there. Even some timber-framed houses have survived from the 15th century. Many windmills appeared in the 13th century and post-medieval mills may be seen at: Pitstone (walk 48); above Turville (walks 4 and 5), where the first one was built in 1293; Cholesbury; Coleshill and Lacey Green (walk 24).

The Chilterns is still described as 'ancient countryside', and retains much of its early history because the often poor soil has not been greatly altered by farming. Hence, the winding, sunken lanes (hollow-ways), 1000-year-old hedges and enclosures can still be seen. The fallow deer introduced for hunting by the Normans are still around e.g. in the deer park at Stonor (walks 7 and 8).

8. From Skirmett to Stonor

Starting Point: Lay-by in Skirmett, near the phone box (776 901).

Access: Reach Skirmett on minor roads e.g. from Lane End on the B482.

Distance: 7½ miles (12km). Can be shortened.

Detail: After a scenic start you pass through a deer park and down past Stonor House. A further climb with fine views and some beech woods are met before the return. You climb 1000ft.

Map: Explorer 3 (W) or Pathfinder 175.

For details of the Stonor estate see walk 7. There may be mud at stage 20.

1. Go N along road towards Fingest. Soon go L along drive to stile. On up path.
2. Go R at wood (fence on your R).
3. L up into wood at its corner. Fork R after 100m.
4. Soon after gentle descent, go ½R down path to wood edge, down field and through trees to road.
5. Turn L along road.
6. Go L up track near house. On past farm. ➘
7. L along road. R along crossing track. Soon ignore side tracks.
8. When track forks L, follow path marked by arrow. Soon through gate and on in Deer Park.
9. Ignore crossing paths. Pass buildings (in valley to your R).
10. Turn L along road.
11. L along path, soon by wire fence on your L. Follow fence up to road.
12. R along road, 100m to stile. Here ½L over field to stile.
13. Go on to stile just L of house.
14. Here R along drive and L between farm and barn, soon by fence on your R, then hedge on your L.

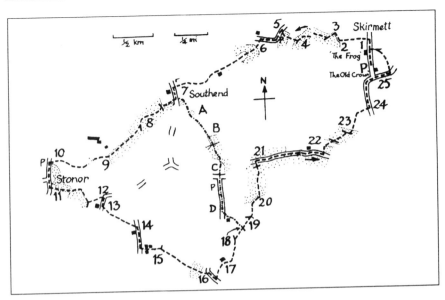

15. Follow poles down field to stile. On up wood, then field to road.

16. R up road and sharp L along drive, passing farm (on your L).

17. On by fence (on your R) to stile. 50m after track turns $\frac{1}{2}$L, go $\frac{1}{2}$R over field to stile. ✎

18. On to field corner. Here go $\frac{1}{2}$L (hedge on your L).

20. At stile go L into wood.

21. R along lane.

22. After vineyard turn L beside fence (on your L). At field go $\frac{1}{2}$R to wood. On down wood. At bottom, go R along track 50m then L down small path out of wood.

23. Along field edge (fence on your R) to stile, and R to road.

24. Go L along road. Keep on at T-junction.

25. Go L just before road bends. Follow fence on your L. It bears L to drive. Along drive to road and R to point 1, or L to phone box at start.

Stonor House

Variations

West of Skirmett (5 miles, 8km, 600ft): Follow 1 to 6. Then L along road and L along crossing track. Where it turns L, go on over field, soon R over stile and L past trees.

A. Go L over next stile and R beside fence.

B. On down wood and up path, bearing slightly away from wood edge. Soon with dark pines by your L.

C. When path gets nearer edge, bear R to stile. L over field. On along lane.

D. ½L along drive. Where concrete drive ends, fork R between hedges. At stile go L over field to its corner. Now follow 19 to 25.

Around Stonor (4½ miles, 7km, 600ft): Park at Stonor as for walk 7. Go S along road past T-junction. Follow 11 to 17. Then L between hedges.

D. Go ½R along road to T-junction.

C. On over field to stile. Into wood along path bearing L, soon by pines on your R. On down and up to stile.

B. Follow fence on your L up field. Near trees go L over stile and R past trees to next stile.

A. R over stile and L. On along track and on over road. Now follow 8 and 9.

Chiltern Geology

Much of the area is chalk, the remains of innumerable sea creatures laid down on the floor of an ancient sea one hundred million years ago. Later on, huge convulsions of the earth threw up the backbone of the Chilterns, running from south-west to north-east with a steep escarpment from Goring to Dunstable and beyond. It is divided by five troughs out of which rivers now flow south-east to reach the Thames. The plateau tops often have a covering of clay with flints put down in the last Ice Age, and there are alluvial deposits in the larger valleys.

Sometimes a siliceous material binds a pebble bed into a solid mass called pudding-stone, for example, on the green at The Lee (walk 32) and at the base of Chesham parish church (near 38). To the untrained eye it may seem like concrete. Some say the earliest name of Chesham meant 'watered valley by a heap of stones', referring to these stones. Pudding-stone has been used to make hand-mills for grinding corn and, when cut and polished, snuff-box lids. It has been used for buildings e.g. an ancient monastic barn at Harmondsworth.

9. Around Bix Bottom

Starting Point: Park near the right-angled bend (717 887) 400m W of Maidensgrove.

Access: This lane leaves the B480 at Stonor.

Distance: 5½ miles (8.5km).

Detail: Bix Bottom is a winding valley which you see from a variety of angles. It has an outstanding nature reserve. You climb 800ft.

Map: Explorer 3 (W) or Pathfinder 175.

The Warburg Nature Reserve is well worth a visit when its many different kinds of orchids are in bloom. You also pass the ruins of a medieval church, last used in 1875.

1. Walk NW, away from Maidensgrove, beside road.
2. 100m past The Five Horseshoes, turn L over stile. Go down two fields (fence on your R).
3. Into third field and R, then L to corner.
4. On over stile then on 10m over next stile. Next go ½L, gently up in trees.
5. On over field. Later make for stile 100m L of farm.
6. Go ½R over field to next stile, then L along track.
7. Where track comes in on L, go sharp R up field to far corner.
8. Here ½R up by wood edge until 150m past house.
9. Then ½R along drive for 100m.
10. At stile, go on over field, passing just R of three pines, to stile.
11. On to road and L along it.
12. Where road turns R, keep on 100m to stile, then ½L along field edge.
13. On into wood. On down fields.
14. Go L along road for 150m and R up track into wood.
15. 100m before house, go L over stile. Ignore stiles on your R.
16. At bottom go R through car park. Go L along grassy strip.
17. At end of strip go on 20m and R up track.

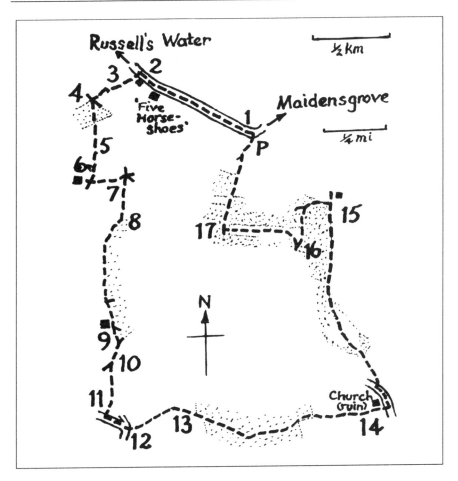

10. North from Henley

Starting Point: By the A4130, N of Henley (755 835).

Access: From the centre of Henley, go N on the A4130 for 1000m and park on the L just after the grass verge widens. A drive on the L runs parallel to the road.

Distance: 3 miles (5km).

Detail: A simple stroll on both sides of the Assendon valley. You climb 400ft.

Map: Explorer 3 (W) or Pathfinder 175.

Lower Assendon in the valley below Lambridge Wood

After enjoying the beeches of Lambridge Wood, there are fine valley views and more in the final descent of the Oxfordshire Way.

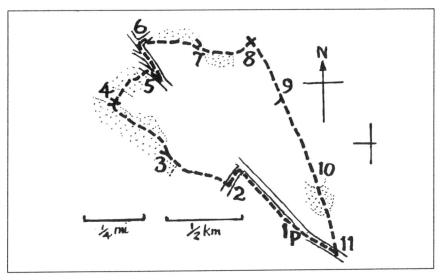

1. Walk NW along this drive. Go L along Lambridge Wood Road.

2. Turn sharp R up shady path. Go on in wood.

3. Near the top, fork R along track that curves L.

4. Go R down path and over drive, with field on your L.

5. Turn R to road junction and sharp L along lane.

6. Turn R up lane and soon R up track.

7. Keep on when track turns sharp L.

8. Turn R along track.

9. Keep on over field when track turns R.

10. Keep on in wood. Bear R, down out of wood.

11. Go R along road.

11. Fawley

Starting Point: Middle Assendon (739 857).

Access: Go NW from Henley on the A4130, fork R along the B480. Park in Middle Assendon, where a minor road goes E off the B480.

Distance: 7 miles (11km). Easily shortened.

Detail: Plenty of views and a fine ridge. You climb 950ft.

Map: Explorer 3 (W) or Pathfinder 175.

After a steep start and fine views, some gentler gradients follow. You pass a free mini-zoo of several unexpected creatures before descending near Fawley Court Farm. After a wooded climb to open hills comes the climax – a superb ridge-top walk S from near Stonor.

1. Go up minor road. Soon go ½R up track.
2. At top of steep rise follow path up open field to hedge with pines.
3. Through hedge and over field to hidden stile just L of house.
4. Over road and along track past house.
5. Look for fence coming in on your L. Here L along fence (on your L).
6. On over track. Along wood edge (on your R).
7. On over road. ⬐
8. Go R along large track.
9. At wood follow fence on your L, thus soon leaving track.
10. On down field to gate and stile in dip.
11. Here go on to road.
12. Here turn sharp L over field. Aim for far end of line of pines.
13. Here over stile and up in wood (fence by your L).
14. As path bears away from fence, watch for hidden stile on R, leaving main path to reach it. On up lane.
15. Turn L at footpath sign (by small, red postbox). Go down to L corner of wood.
16. Up shallow valley in fields to sheds.
17. Go through gate, over track and through gate (slightly to R). Follow L edge of field. Having curved round to the L you reach a corner.

18. Here cross stile and go R along drive.

19. Over road and $\frac{1}{2}$R to stile in fence, 30m up from trees.

20. Down field edge to small gate.

21. Down path in wood and over track.

22. Down road. R at T-junction.

23. After 100m keep on up farm road.

24. After pond and last house, go $\frac{1}{2}$L over stile towards L of two houses.

25. At stile go $\frac{1}{3}$R to stile just R of R-hand house.

26. Here L along road 150m, R along track 150m. Bear L along ridge track.

27. When track reaches open field, bear R by fence down to wood.

28. In wood, bear L along path near its top edge.

29. On down field and $\frac{1}{2}$L along road to start.

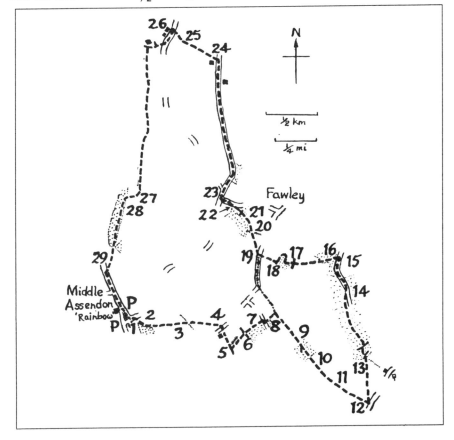

The final descent of the long ridge to Middle Assendon

Variations

Shorter walk (5 miles, 8km, 650ft): Follow 1 to 7, then go L along large track. On along road 300m.

19. Opposite drive go ½L to stile in fence, 30m up from trees. Now follow 20 to 29.

12. Hambleden

Starting Point: Hambleden car park (785 866).

Access: The village can be reached by turning off the A4155 at Mill End, 3 miles N from Henley.

Distance: 8 miles (13km). Can be shortened.

Detail: A fine exploration of the Hambleden valley area. You climb 900ft.

Map: Explorer 3 (W) or Pathfinder 175.

After a short climb through beeches and fields to Greenlands (where W.H. Smith once lived) you head N up a valley and over a wooded ridge back to the Hambleden valley. On its other side you meet a variety of fine views and beech woods. The charming village has a Tudor manor house and a 13th-century church which is full of interest: a 12th- century or late Saxon font, a carved oak altar and a memorial to Sir Cope D'Oyley's family (the children holding skulls died before their parents).

Hambleden with its church and manor

1. From the car park turn L down road.
2. When beside the church, go ½L along road.
3. At road junction, go on up path. Ignore paths forking L.
4. When path starts to drop, ignore R turn.
5. Over paths at wood edge. On over field by fence.
6. On over tracks to road. At once R along track past farm. On along valley bottom.
7. At crossing track, go on up.
8. Fork R into wood.
9. Turn R up track, which goes R after 20m.
10. When track levels at T-junction, go L.
11. At next cross track turn R along it. Keep near wood edge. Ignore side turnings. Soon track is surfaced.
12. At sharp R turn go on through gap and ½R down field to gap.
13. Go along lane opposite gap. ⮑
14. Soon go L with road.
15. Straight on along track where road goes R.
16. Turn R along lane to wood.
17. Here go R, up, near wood edge, over stile and on in field to wood.
18. Here go L, up, by wood edge. On into wood at stile.
20. Up field to farm and lane.
21. Go R down road 30m and fork L into wood. Ignore track going ½L to wood edge.
22. 400m later fork ⅓L along path which gently rises at first.
23. Go L at crossing track, soon leaving wood.
24. At road go R, and soon R again.
25. At footpath sign bear L along top edge of wood. Soon track leaves edge and turns ½R.
26. On over cross track.
27. On when larger track is joined. Follow it L out of wood.
28. R down track to road.
29. At road go L, and L again to car park (or R to 2).

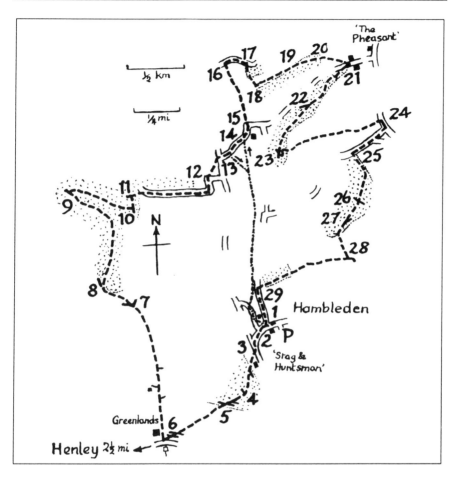

Variations

East of Hambleden (5½ miles, 8.5km, 450ft): Follow 1 and go through the churchyard, passing just L of church. Go on 100m along road, then R at signpost along clear path through fields, gardens and fields. Go R at lane and follow 14 to 29.

West of Hambleden (5 miles, 8km, 500ft): Follow 1 to 13. Soon go ⅔R over two fields and stile (40m L of field corner). Go R along path. On through fields, gardens, and fields. Bear R to signpost 120m R of church. Go L along road, through churchyard (pass R of church) and gate. Go L along road.

13. Near Marlow

Starting Point: Marlow Common (829 973).

Access: Take the minor road from Marlow through Bovingdon Green. At a junction turn L for 100m and park beside the wooded common.

Distance: 6½ miles (10.5km). Can be slightly shorter.

Detail: Plenty of open views and a splendid ridge near the end. You climb 900ft.

Map: Explorer 3 (E) or Pathfinder 175.

Apart from the usual Chiltern features such as beech woods, you also look down on the most attractive Bluey's Farm at stage 16. There may be some mud at point 20 and on the common. To avoid the latter, go back to the junction, turn L, then go L along track to reach point 2 after passing last house.

1. Walk back towards junction and go sharp L along path in wood. Keep on along main path, following arrows – thus forking R, soon forking L and keeping on where arrow shows junction with path coming in from L.
2. On over track and between fences. At wood edge go ½R down field to stile near barn. Then ½L up next field (hedge on your R).
3. Over stile near houses and along path between fences.
4. R along road 60m and ½L up field to stile 40m L of field corner and double pole.
5. Go R along road.
6. At Woodend House go on along track. Down field (hedge on your L).
7. Near bottom go L over stile (hedge on your L). Later go on over track (ignoring stile on L).
8. When hedge goes L, you go ½R, aiming just R of double poles.
9. Go ½L over stiles (now fence on your R).
10. Turn R along road and R at T-junction.
11. At next junction go sharp L along track, soon bearing R. At farm go on down and up wide grass strip. ↘
12. At top go L through gate and by pines. After a short climb, fork L to gate and on down field, soon by hedge on your L. On along wood edge.

13. Go R to stile and ½R up rough field, later walking just below its top edge.
14. Into wood and L up its edge to stile. Over stile and R along wood edge.
15. Over stile and down track.
16. After pines go on over stile (hedge on your L).
17. On along wood edge for 50m then L over stile and up into wood. Soon join track.
18. Near bottom end of wood fork L to its corner. Here bear L up track.
19. Bear R along road.
20. On through farm, over field and down ridge.
21. On over road.
22. Go R along road and L at junction.

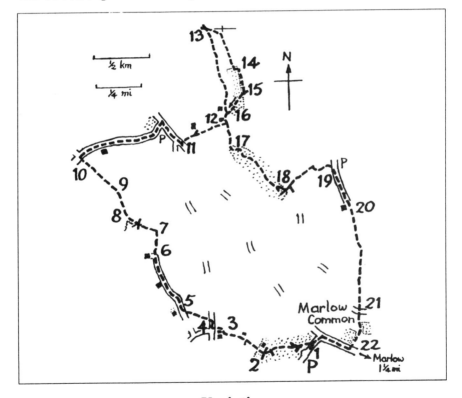

Variation

Shorter walk (5½ miles, 8.5km, 800ft): Follow 1 to 11, then at top go R (hedge on your L) and follow 17 to 22.

14. Cookham Dean

Starting Point: Car park N of Cookham Dean (870 861).

Access: From Marlow, cross the river and fork L along Quarry Wood Road. At top turn L and fork L. Keep on to car park.

Distance: $4\frac{1}{2}$ miles (7km).

Detail: Look down on the Thames, with a backdrop of Chiltern hills, on this easy stroll. You climb 450ft.

Map: Explorer 3 (E) or Pathfinder 175.

The river can be reached by a short detour. It inspired the classic tale *Wind in the Willows,* in which Wild Wood was actually Quarry Wood, and Toad Hall was nearby Cliveden.

1. Keep on along lane or a parallel path which returns to lane.
2. Sharp L down track. Soon R along path.
3. Go down track. After gate, stay on main track.

The Thames, with the hills of the walk beyond

4. Keep on at signpost until opposite board walk. (Go L at signpost to visit river if you wish.) Here sharp R up steep path. On when gradient eases.

5. Later bear L up to stile. On along field edge. Later go $\frac{1}{3}$R between fences.

6. On over lane. L along lane.

7. On 80m past crossroads and R over stile.

8. Bear L along road.

9. At road junction, cross green to pub sign. Go $\frac{1}{3}$L along drive and then path (just R of pub).

10. At stile, go $\frac{1}{3}$L down and up field.

11. Over road and R along parallel path just inside wood.

12. At road junction go L along road which bends R.

13. At end of houses go R along path; soon L along path in wood, later with steep ground on L.

14. On along drive 30m and $\frac{1}{2}$L to road.

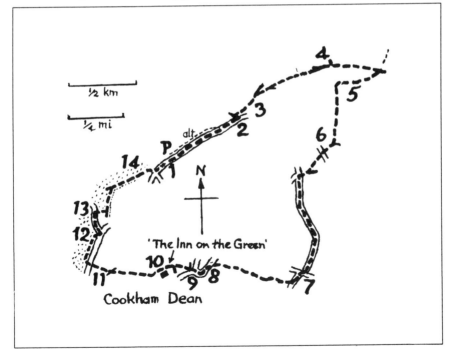

15. Sheepridge

Starting Point: Opposite The Crooked Billet (883 895).

Access: This inn is about 1000m along the lane that goes N off the A4155 at Well End (884 882).

Distance: 4½ miles (7km).

Detail: An easy walk with two open ridges. You climb 500ft.

Map: Explorer 3 (E) or Pathfinder 175.

The ridges give good Thames-ward views, and there is some attractive woodland.

1. Walk up road. As it bends L, turn R up steps.

2. On over stile at top, soon bearing L.

3. At scout hut go R. Soon R between fences. On down path.

4. On over road to houses.

Woodman's Cottage, Sheepridge

5. Here sharp R along track.

6. On to wood (where hedge bends R). L along edge to stile. Here $\frac{1}{2}$R along path in wood, soon going on over track.

7. At track go L 5m and R along narrower path in more open, heathy land. Soon fork R (along crossing path).

8. On over track. At junction go $\frac{1}{2}$R, soon crossing track, then on in wood with field on your R.

9. On along field edge.

10. At gate before farm, go L 30m to cross stile then R along field edge.

11. Go R up lane and R along road.

12. After slight descent go R over stile and along ridge (hedge on your L). After stile, hedge is on your R.

13. Go L at path junction, and soon down drive.

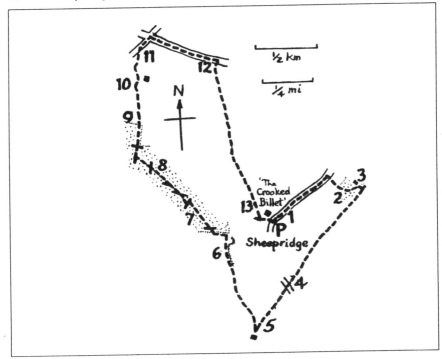

16. From Stokenchurch to Radnage

Starting Point: Car park by King's Arms (761 963)

Access: Go W from High Wycombe to Stokenchurch on the A40.

Distance: 8 miles (13km). Can be shortened.

Detail: A walk abounding in good views. You climb 1200ft.

Map: Explorer 3 (W) or Pathfinder 165.

At stage 9 you have the choice of a valley track (can be muddy) or a ridge-top lane. There may be mud between points 18 and 19. Radnage Church has a Norman tower (AD1200), a Saxon font, fragments of medieval murals and a fine nave roof (AD1470). Stokenchurch Church (13th century) also has a Norman tower.

1. Walk past the L end of King's Arms and shops. R along road, L along Church Path. It goes L 10m, then R. At road go R along it, soon L.

2. R at signpost. On with hedge on your R. Over stile and down with fence on your L.

3. At bottom go up field, eventually reaching hedge on your L.

4. On into wood (near its edge). Go L at bottom.

5. On out of wood. Soon ⅔R beside trees, kept on your L.

6. At farm ½R and soon ½L along field (fence on your R).

7. Turn R along track. At junction turn L up track, which soon bears R.

8. On over field into wood (100m R of its end).

9. Down wood 50m and R along valley track.

10. Watch for stile and go L over it, up field and R along lane. ↝

11. At signpost by houses go sharp R along drive which bears L past bungalow. On down path, soon hedge on your L.

12. Through gap in field corner. On down past house (on your right) to road. Down it 150m then L 100m along road and R over field to church.

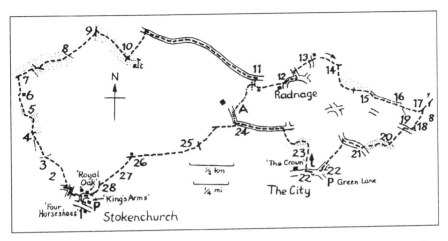

13. On through churchyard. Over steps in wall and ½R down field to stile. On to next stile. Here go ½R over field to stile at wood edge.

14. Go along by wood edge through fields.

15. At end of wood fork L by wide hedge on L and fence on R.

16. When hedge bears R, go ½L through gap and up between fences.

17. Go R down track.

18. Leave track at next iron steps. Down field to stile. R along road.

19. Soon turn L across field.

20. Turn R up wood, mainly near L edge.

21. Go R down lane. As it goes R, turn L up track.

22. Turn R along road. Soon R along path.

23. Into wood, bearing L. Out down drive. L along lane. ↝

24. When it goes R to farm, go L on track which at once goes R. At sign go ½L up field to its top. Here cross track and go L by hedge on your L.

25. On in next field. 200m before house go L through gap and R along track.

26. At house go ½L over field to pole (or on 100m and along field edge).

27. On to stile and up L side of shallow valley with trees on your R.

28. L along lane. At Royal Oak go R along road, L past shops and L to start.

Variations

To avoid lane: Stay on valley track at stage 9 until beyond wood.

A. At sign go sharp L up field to hedge gap, ½R over stile and by hedge on your R.

11. At stiles go R over drive, ½R past bungalow (on your R) and down path, soon a hedge on your L. Now follow 12 to 29.

Radnage (4 miles, 6km, 700ft): Park in quiet side roads in The City (786 967), W of Stokenchurch, reached by a minor road off the A40. From the junction with Green Lane go W (towards The Crown). Soon go R along path. Follow stage 23. Then go R towards farm. At sign go ½R up field to hedge gap, ½R over stile and by hedge on your R. Now follow stage 11 onwards in the above variation.

Stokenchurch (5 miles, 8km, 650ft): Follow 1 to 10.

11. At signpost by houses go sharp R along drive. Soon go R over stiles and drive, then L by hedge down to gap. Down field to drive, and L along it.

24. R along track at junction. At sign go ½L up field to its top. Cross track and go L by hedge (on your L). Follow 26 to 29.

17. Bledlow

Starting Point: Lay-by at 784 005.

Access: From the B4009, turn S at a crossroads and proceed for nearly 2 miles (3km), passing Bledlow. When 200m past a R bend, the lay-by is on your R by a footpath sign.

Distance: 8 miles (12.5km).

Detail: A largely open walk with wide views and various items of interest along the way. You climb 1100ft.

Map: Explorer 2 and 3 (W) or Pathfinder 165.

Early in this walk you may enjoy the abundant wild flowers on the small, isolated Lodge Hill. Next you cross Bledlow Ridge, encountering Radnage Church before the climb to Chinnor Hill. There you will find a nature reserve with orchids and Bronze Age burial mounds. Bledlow has an attractive 16th-century inn (The Lions) and a church (12th to 14th century) with interesting wall paintings, font and S doorway. Near the church you can visit the Lyde, a deep ravine and source of a river. There could be mud at times at 4 and 5 (avoided by going up to road), and 8 to 9.

Place Names

Many place names are Anglo-Saxon, and their endings describe the landscape. Long winding valleys have the ending **-den** e.g. Assenden, Hambleden, Hampden, Hughenden. Steep-sided valleys have **-combe** e.g. Swyncombe, Coombe (below Coombe Hill). Ridges which jut out have **-hoe** e.g. Ivinghoe. Hills with a flat top and one or two rounded ends have **-or** e.g. Chinnor, Stonor, Pednor. Open country has an ending **-feld**, thus Turville or thyrre feld refers to the flattish area between Northend, Turville Heath and Southend. The ending **-ham** for homesteads is probably pre-Anglo-Saxon e.g. Burnham.

1. Over stile opposite lay-by and SE across two fields, towards Lodge Hill.
2. Through gate and R along path, soon climbing hill.
3. At 4-way signpost, go R down and up fields, later with fence on your R.
4. On up lane.
5. Go L at signposted path between shrubs and fence. On along lower edge of fields.
6. R up lane. L along enclosed path. On over field (hedge by your R).
7. On over stile, now hedge on your L. On along drive to road.
8. Over road and on along path.
9. Ignore path going off down on L just inside wood. Follow path which soon curves L to reach open ground (with shrubs). Here, down path, keeping near trees on your R.
10. Soon there are trees on your L, too. Just as they end, go L down path to stile. Over three fields to church (in trees) and $\frac{1}{2}$L through churchyard to road.
11. Over road and on across field to R of large gate.
12. R along road and on along drive where road goes L.
13. On along track where drive goes R.
14. At stile go on over field. Make for far hedge going up to house.
15. Follow this hedge (keep it on your R).
16. On over stile, through wood and along field edge to road.
17. Here R along road. L at bend along track past buildings.
18. Here go L to road and R along it.
19. At bend go R along Hill Top Lane.
20. Just past Hill Top Cottage and car park, go L and soon R along track into wood.
21. At open ground go $\frac{1}{2}$L to fence and $\frac{1}{2}$R by it. (You could visit the nature reserve and rejoin our route a little lower down.)
22. Soon path gently descends among trees. Later walk on L bank of sunken path.
23. Bear R to signpost by house. Down track (Swan's Way) with fields on R.
24. Where track turns $\frac{1}{2}$R, go on over field to house and $\frac{1}{2}$R along road.
25. At sign go R along path, soon by hedge on your L.
26. On over track and field. Down through trees and up.
27. Over two stiles and $\frac{1}{2}$L by fence (on your L). 10m before fence turns R, go L through gate and R by fence. L at road.

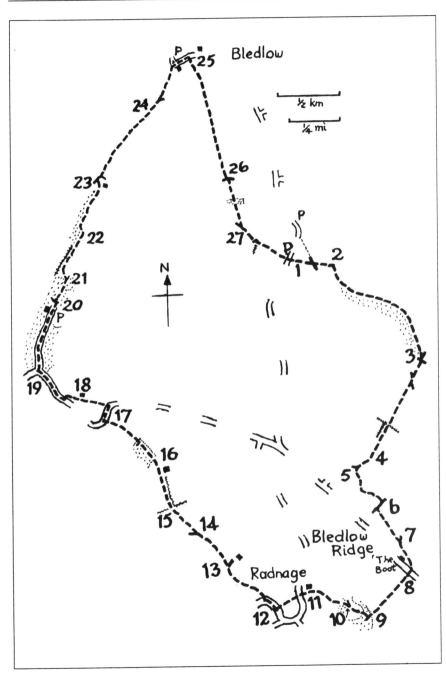

18. Bradenham to Bledlow Ridge

Starting Point: Bradenham (828 972).

Access: From W Wycombe on the A40, go N along the A4010, turn R into the village and park opposite the church.

Distance: 8 miles (12.5km). Can be shortened.

Detail: Plenty of extensive views on this walk from a beautiful, unspoilt village. You climb 950ft.

Map: Explorer 3 or Pathfinder 165.

Bradenham has cottages, farms, manor (home of Disraeli's father) and church (15th-century tower; Norman S doorway), all set round a large green.

1. Go W to the A4010 and R for 50m.
2. L through gate and up field to stile. Over railway and on up field to stile in hedge.
3. Slant gently R up next field. Aim to reach trees ahead about 70m L of their R-hand edge.
4. On in wood.
5. On over path.
6. Bear R along track. Soon ½R along drive.
7. Over road and up hill. ↘
8. L at road.
9. R at crossroads, along drive for 150m, then L over stile and field to stile at hedge corner.
10. Here on up field edge (hedge on your L).
11. Over stile and ⅓R up next field. Over stile between fences to road.
12. Go R along road 100m, and R along rough road.
13. At its end go ⅓L over stile and follow hedge (on your R) to stiles.
14. Here over L stile and along field top, between hedge and fence.

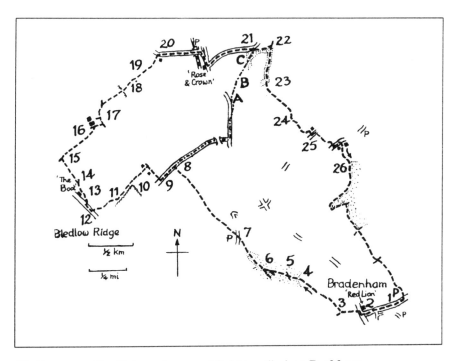

15. On over stile. R down lane and field to stile just R of farm.

16. Over stile, L to farm, R along drive and L at drive junction.

17. Where drive goes L, keep on along track for 100m, then fork R along track. At hedge, over stile to pylon.

18. On over stile just L of pylon (hedge on your R).

19. Near houses, bear L along field edge to stile at road.

20. R along road, R after bridge, R along main road then L along road until it bends L.

21. Here go R over stile and at once L over stile. Up field by wood edge.

22. At top, R over stile and along in wood.

23. Leave wood. Keep on along field edges (hedge on your L), down ridge.

24. Follow track after hedge stops. At fence go R 40m to road.

25. L along road. Soon R between buildings along grass track (fence on your L).

26. Follow track along wood edge, thus later bearing L steeply up, then R gently down. On to Bradenham. R along road.

Variation

Bradenham (5½ miles, 9km, 700ft): Follow 1 to 7, then R at road and L at main road.

A. Fork R along rough road for 80m, R up steps and ½L over field to stile just L of pole.

B. On to next two stiles. On up field to farm gate at far top corner.

C. On over stile to two stiles by lane. Turn R over stile and up field by wood edge. Now follow 22 to 26.

Chiltern Woodlands

In medieval times woods represented the largest natural renewable resource for fuel and construction of houses, fences, etc. Beech was the commonest woodland tree, with oak coming second (oak was useful for house building). These woods were more open than present-day woods, with trees in various stages of growth. Below the larger trees, coppice trees were cut right down every six years or so to provide poles and firewood. Sometimes trees were periodically pollarded, i.e. cut back to about three metres to prevent animals nibbling new shoots.

Wood was a useful export to London, via the Thames, as the town rapidly grew in the 16th and 17th centuries. But there was a decline in wooded areas, as coal became a cheaper fuel than wood. Fortunately for the present day survival of the beechwoods, the late 18th century showed a rapid growth in chair-making. In a large area centred on High Wycombe, bodgers turned chair-legs etc on their primitive lathes, while small factories completed the construction. This resulted in most of the woods having more trees left to grow tall and fewer small trees. The work of the bodgers died out around 1900 when mass-production by machine-tools took over. Thankfully these woods remain to enhance the present day landscape. The Forestry Commission has planted conifers in a few places, but recent planning seems to favour a return to beech woods.

19. West of West Wycombe

Starting Point: Car park on the A4010 at W Wycombe (826 947).

Access: Go 150m up the A4010 from its junction with the A40.

Distance: 8 miles (13km).

Detail: Many scenic ridges are walked or crossed on this tour, and one winding 'bottom', with some beech wood sections. You climb 950ft.

Map: Explorer 3 or Pathfinder 165 and 175.

The attractive National Trust village has many old buildings (from around the 16th century). Nearby West Wycombe Park (18th-century house and grounds) is open to the public. Church Hill, above the village, was the site of an Iron Age defended settlement. There was once a village up there, but now there is only the Mausoleum of 1752 and the church with its golden ball (big enough to hold several people) and unusual interior. Strange occurrences in this region are likely to be due to Sir Francis Dashwood (1708-1781), founder of the notorious Hell Fire Club. In the caves and passages

The Ridgeway

This long-distance path starts near Avebury and runs 85 miles to Ivinghoe Beacon. The route was officially approved in 1972. The western half follows a line of chalk downs with open fields bearing crops or sheep. The Chiltern half is more wooded and the better walking country, though with somewhat less archaeological interest.

In the Bronze Age, or possibly before, a trading route was used from Dorset to the coast of Norfolk. Parts of this can be walked by linking up the Wessex Ridgeway, Ridgeway, Icknield Way and Peddars Way. Around 1800, the Enclosure Acts defined the course of the Ridgeway – a wide way of twelve or more metres, with hedges on each side. Since then some of it has been used for roads, in which case the long-distance path uses a more enjoyable route.

In this book the Ridgeway is first met near Swyncombe (walk 1). About twenty miles of the most scenic stretches are covered, including parts of walks 2, 3, 17, 28, 29, 30, 42 and 43, and its splendid finale at Ivinghoe Beacon (47).

excavated under the hill it was rumoured that diabolical events took place. To find out more, buy a ticket to the caves. There may be muddy sections from points 8 to 10.

1. Return to the junction. Go SW for 200m along A40 towards Oxford.

2. Then, near lane on L, go ½R up two fields.

3. On up third field (first a hedge on your L) to stile at wood edge.

4. On in wood.

5. As wood ends, go 30m R along track, then L along track.

6. Go L then down by fence or hedge on your L in two fields; fence on your R in last field. On into farmyard.

7. R through small gate and along path with long barn on your R. Soon on along track.

8. At trees take R fork over fields to gates. On in trees along valley bottom. Soon ignore R fork up.

9. At display board track bears R.

10. 30m before wood on R ends, go sharp R up path, soon forking L to stay about 5m from wood edge up to its top.

11. Here on up field (hedge on your L) to farm.

12. On through farm and ⅓R over field to road.

13. L along road 100m, then R along path down and up to road.

14. L along road.

15. Go R up just inside wood edge and on to road (hedge on your L).

16. R along road.

17. L along Scrubbs Lane and on down fields (hedge on your R) to road.

18. L down road. Just after farm go R to stile and ½L up field.

19. On into wood at top corner of field. ½R on drive along ridge.

20. On over crossing path at end of pines.

21. On over grass, passing just L of trees on L of Golden Ball. Bear R by these trees to Mausoleum.

22. L down line of trees, almost to road.

23. Go R past caves' entrance (on your R) and on by path to start.

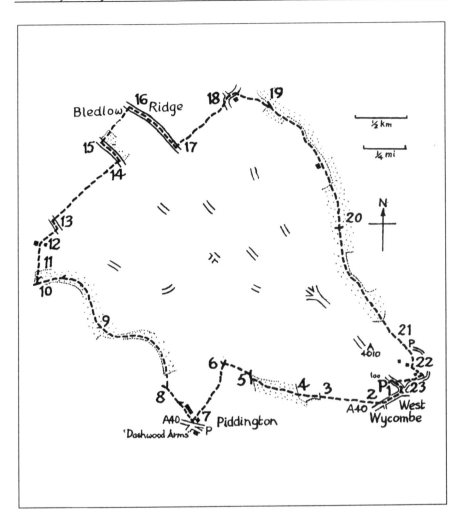

20. West Wycombe to Bradenham

Starting Point: Car park on the A4010 at W Wycombe (826 947).

Access: Go 150m up the A4010 from its junction with the A40.

Distance: 8 miles (12.5km). Can be shortened.

Detail: Another chance to enjoy the two villages and their delightful surroundings. You climb 1300ft.

Map: Explorer 3 (E) or Pathfinder 165 and 175.

At point 24 you pass Chawley Farm, an Elizabethan building. For notes on West Wycombe, see walk 19; for Bradenham, see walk 18.

West Wycombe Hill

Variation

Note: this 'variation' is included here so that the main walk text and map can be presented on facing pages.

Shorter walk (5 miles, 7.5km, 600ft): Follow 1 to 10, then L along road, soon forking R. After pub go R over the A40, ½L along track and through small gate, past long barn on your R. Follow 15 to 23, then R along main road.

A. Soon L up track. It narrows and bears R along wood edge.

B. Ignore L fork 50m before open grass. Then bear R to start.

The BBONT

The nature reserves of BBONT (pronounced 'bee-bont') cover Berks, Bucks and Oxfordshire, and preserve a vital selection of habitats which otherwise might be lost. For enquiries contact BBONT, 3 Church Cowley Road, Rose Hill, Oxford, OX4 3JR (tel. 01865 775 476). In visiting them it is vital not to pick the flowers or otherwise disturb the reserve, and to stay on the paths when they are marked.

Some of the downland reserves (often with beech woods) open to visitors include Aston Clinton (887 107, near walk 42), Chinnor Hill (17), Chequers (29), Dancersend and The Crong (900 095 and 904 088, near walks 42 and 43) and Grangelands (28). At Hartslock (616 796) near Goring a warden keeps an eye on the monkey orchids. Homefield Wood (814 867) near Marlow and Pitstone Hill (47) are also worth a visit. Best of all is the Warburg reserve (9), with an exceptional variety of orchids including the fly orchid.

Birdwatchers are catered for at Weston Turville Reservoir (859 095) and three other non-BBONT reservoirs north of Tring. Apart from their marsh flora, they are important for wintering wildfowl and birds on passage e.g. waders and terns. In 1938, little ringed plovers chose one of them to begin nesting in Britain.

A similar selection of birds can be seen from various hides at the exceptional College Lake wildlife centre, two miles north-east of Tring, by the B488. Visitors are welcome, but need to buy a permit on arrival. It is a worked-out chalk quarry and there are water plants and chalk downland plants to be seen, exhibits to enjoy and an area where cornfield weeds are grown. Many birds breed there e.g. lapwing, redshank and little ringed plover. It's certainly well worth a visit.

Kingfishers may be seen here and in other watery places. Firecrests nest in Wendover Woods, and there is a hide and waymarked trail in which they may be seen on stage 13 of walk 42. Red kites were reintroduced in 1989 and are still spreading. They may be seen on the first 22 walks.

1. Return to the junction. Go SW for 200m along A40 towards Oxford.

2. Turn L up lane.

3. 50m before top fork R.

4. Near farm, go on to pass by pylon.

5. Follow hedge on your R past hedge gap.

6. Fork R to mast, then go R over field into wood.

7. On emerging, keep along hedge (on your L) then beside wood (on your R) until you come to stile.

8. Here go into wood. Soon out and L up road.

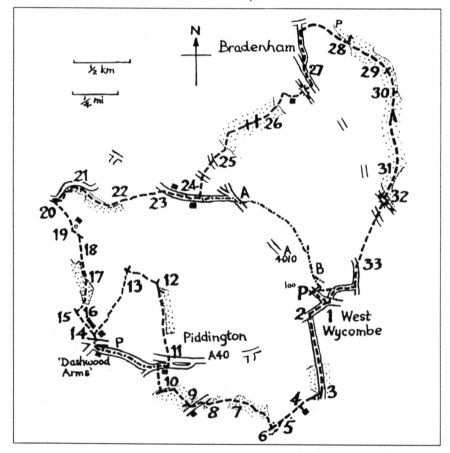

9. Near farm, fork ½R along track. After 50m turn R over stile and down wood. Near wood bottom, path bears L.

10. When you reach wood edge, cross stile. Down field to gate just L of single house. ↘

11. R 80m along road, then L over main road and up track.

12. L along track just after passing top corner of wood.

13. L over stile, down by fence or hedge (on your L in two fields, then on your R). On into farmyard.

14. R through small gate and along path (long barn on your R). Soon on along track.

15. R through small 'gate'. Up by fence.

16. Enter the wood.

17. On emerging, bear L along wood edge to hedge gap.

18. Here go up and cross stile. On to far field corner.

19. On between pond and hedge. Then ½L to follow poles to road.

20. R at road and very soon R into field. Go along L edge of field.

21. Just after going R at field corner, turn into wood along path (lane below on L). As lane turns L, path bears R along lower wood edge (inside wood). Follow fence as it bears L to stile.

22. Here over fields towards farm with pylon behind it.

23. R at road. ↘

24. L over stile opposite farm. The path crosses two small roads.

25. Climb hill up into wood. Path winds upwards. When it levels, cross over wider track and keep on to a second cross track.

26. Here keep on. Bear L down drive. L along road.

27. Go ½R along lane. 50m before road junction, go R along track.

28. At sharp L bend (10m before signpost) go on in same direction as before bend (SE) up narrow path. Keep on in beeches. Follow arrows. Later, on along clear track.

29. Ignore cross track in slight dip. On up path.

30. Go ½R along track. Go on along path when track turns ½L.

31. At wood end path goes ½R down by fence (on your L) to railway.

32. On to road and on up to far corner of field.

33. Here go down lane and soon R along lane. Cut over grass to start.

21. West Wycombe to Wheeler End

Starting Point: Car park on the A4010 at W Wycombe (826 947).

Access: Go 150m up the A4010 from its junction with the A40.

Distance: 7½ miles (12km). Can be shortened.

Detail: Yet another good walk in this area, not repeating the other walks until the last mile or so. You climb 1000ft.

Map: Explorer 3 or Pathfinder 165 and 175.

At first you go through woods and hills of the West Wycombe Estate. Beyond Wheeler End Common there is a fine, open ridge, and later on another one makes a fine finale.

1. Return to the junction. Go SW for 200m along A40 towards Oxford.
2. Then turn L up lane. Bear L at top.
3. Just before thatched cottage, go R and on by hedge on your L.
4. At bottom, over stile and R along field edge. Go L at its corner.
5. After 50m go R into wood and L near its edge. On along track.
6. Fork L out of wood near its end. R up track (hedge on your R).
7. Near top of rise go sharp R along short track and L over fields (hedge on your L). Over stile and down to wood.
8. On into wood, out by stiles and over field.
9. Into wood (follow arrows), soon downwards. At bottom, on up 100m.
10. When path bends R, go L to stile by gate. Over and up field.
11. Aim for gate and stile in front of barns. Over stile and ½R to road just R of barn.
12. L along road. ⌇
13. After road bends L and starts to descend, go R along grass track in bracken (opposite Harodaim). Go over two crossing tracks, then L to white post L of phone box.
14. Over road and along lane.
15. 80m after lane turns R, go ½L over stile to wood. At stile go on in wood.
16. On leaving wood, go R along track.
17. At wood corner, go L down field. At arrow go R into wood. Soon go ½L down small path to bottom.

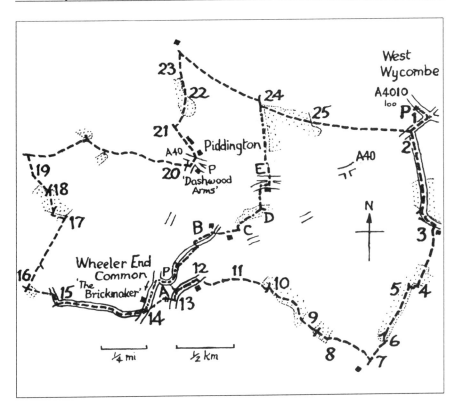

18. Here go L 5m, then R up by wood on your L.

19. At top, ½R down to track and R along it. Keep hedge on your R.

20. Go L along lane, over road, and ½L along track and through small gate, passing long barn on your R.

21. R through small 'gate', up by fence on your L and into wood.

22. On emerging, bear L along wood edge to hedge gap.

23. Here go up and cross stile. On to far field corner. Sharp R along field edge. Soon along track. ↘

24. Bear R when track comes in on L. Soon L into wood.

25. On over field, soon with hedge on your R. On down fields and L along road (or to continue walk go R along lane, bear L at top and follow 3 onwards).

Near Piddington

Variations

Shorter walk (5 miles, 8km, 850ft): Follow 1 to 12, then go ½R along stony track.

A. Soon R along Piddington Lane. Over stile on R to walk near lane. Over gaps (or stiles if any) to walk near lane (now on your R).

B. Over stile by house, R over lane and along track past farm. Soon on over field (hedge on your R) to corner. Over stile and L to wood.

C. Follow path ½R down wood to lower edge and stile.

D. Over stile and field to gate just L of single house.

E. Go R 80m, L over main road and on up track.

24. At top corner of wood, turn R into wood and follow 25.

Wheeler End (5½ miles, 8.5km, 600ft): At Piddington, leave the A40 and drive to Wheeler End. Park on L at top of hill (804 933). Walk SW along road past the Brickmaker and go ½R along lane. Follow 15 to 23. Then bear R when track comes in on L.

E. On over road, R 80m along lane and L up field to stile at wood edge.

D. Over stile and R along path, soon climbing to top corner.

C. Over stile, up 50m to stile and R along field edge. Near houses, go on between hedges to lane.

B. Over lane and L over stile. Keep by lane, cross it at gaps (or stiles if any) and R, still by lane. Over stile and L along lane.

The Ancient Chilterns

Hunter-gatherers roamed the area from around 100 000BC whenever an Ice Age receded. After the last Ice Age trees spread across the landscape, and man was back again. By 4000BC farmsteads appeared. Large areas were cleared for fuel, buildings, crops and grazing, and the Icknield Way, a trading route, ran along the edge of the Chilterns, linking Norfolk and the Salisbury Plain. In summer, the Lower Icknield Way was used, running below the escarpment. When this became waterlogged, a less direct route along the Upper Icknield Way was used. Flint was mined on Pitstone Hill (walk 47). Barrows marking burial places of tribal chieftains appeared e.g. at Whiteleaf Hill (walks 28 and 29). Still more are to be found from the Bronze Age e.g. the Five Knolls (walk 49) and above Chinnor (walk 17).

In the Iron Age, from 900BC, the population increased; one settlement on Chinnor Hill kept pigs, ponies, and primitive cattle. This gave rise to a number of hill forts, the one at Ivinghoe being one of the earliest in Britain (walk 47). There is one at Boddington Hill (hidden in woods near walk 42), and at Pulpit Hill (near walk 29; reached with the help of a track going SE off the Ridgeway at 830 053).

Grim's Ditch was a major construction work with several sections: from Lacey Green to Hampden (walk 27) with an interesting 90-degree bend; from The Lee to Cholesbury; and from Pitstone to Ivinghoe (walk 47). Its purpose is uncertain – maybe it marked a boundary.

22. Hughenden

Starting Point: Naphill (848 962).

Access: Leave the A4128 2 miles (3km) N of High Wycombe at a roundabout. Go on and soon L, uphill, towards Naphill. At the top, where the road bends R, go on to the end of a lane.

Distance: 7 miles (11km). Can be shortened.

Detail: An introduction to the pleasant Hughenden Valley, with more views as you approach W Wycombe. You climb 900ft.

Map: Explorer 3 (E) or Pathfinder 165 and 175.

The walk passes Hughenden Manor (National Trust), the home of Disraeli. Part of this is now a museum with his pictures, books, furniture, etc. He is buried in the nearby church. At point 20 you can see the Pedestal (1752), an odd signpost which does not name the three towns to which the roads lead. Expect some mud in wet seasons e.g. at 7, 10 and 26.

1. Walk back (NE) along lane. At road junction, go on down road.
2. Soon after it bends R, go L (30m after drive) down path in field.
3. Over stile by wood edge and down by fence on your R. On down rough road.
4. At bottom, go R 50m along road, and L over field.
5. Go up drive. Soon fork R up track 50m, then go R between fences.
6. Go ½L along track to road.
7. Cross road and bear R at footpath sign. Go on along top edge of fields. Later keep just below shrubs.
8. Through gate at field corner and down path.
9. Over stile, R 70m and L along field edge.
10. After barn go on to stile, over it, and R down path.
11. At road go L 50m, then R along drive and on grass to pass just L of house and church. Make for drive at a point midway between two houses, and go L up it. ↯
12. Just past Hughenden Manor, where drive bends L, go on **down** path which at once bears R. Keep on down where path crosses yours.

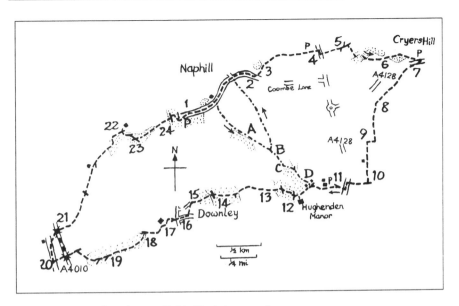

13. Out of wood and over field. On into wood.

14. At wide crossing track, go on gently up.

15. At lane, go ½L up path and R along road.

16. At T-junction go on 60m and fork R at signpost. Along L edge of field, over stile and bear L, soon between hedge and fence.

17. Go past school entrance and R at path sign.

18. At wood go ½L along its top edge.

19. At vague fork, fork R down clear path. Later again fork R down. On down field to stile and L along lane.

20. Go R at road. By buildings, go ½R over field to gate and under railway. On up field (fence on your L).

21. Bear ½L with fence. At dip, go on up to barn. On along lane.

22. At fork near buildings, go R into wood. Soon bear L, then fork R down.

23. Go L up valley track. On over field to stile.

24. Here go on to reach track, L along it 10m and R along path. It soon bears R to run parallel to a track, then bears L to end of lane.

Variations

Western Half (5 miles, 8km, 650ft): Go back along lane. After it starts climbing, turn sharp R over fields by hedge on your R.

A. At dip, where wood bears R, keep on over field to stile 50m R of large tree.

B. Over stile and R along by hedge on your R.

C. At wood go ½L for 100m to field corner and on into wood. Soon along wood edge.

D. Go ½L when fence goes L. Go up drive and follow 12 to 24.

Eastern Half (4 miles, 6km, 500ft): Again take the road to Naphill. After it bends R at the top, park in the rough Trees Road, the second turning on the L. Follow 4 to 11 then, at drive, go up path just L of Park Cottage.

D. Soon walk by fence (on your R) along wood edge, then back into wood. Ignore crossing path 50m before leaving wood. Go ⅓L out of wood, along its edge.

C. Over stile, R along stony track and R down road. Follow 2 and 3.

23. Around Speen

Starting Point: Speen (840 998).

Access: From High Wycombe go N on the A4128. Go straight on along minor roads at the roundabout. Park in quiet side road, e.g. Studridge Lane, N of the road through Speen.

Distance: 7½ miles, 12km. Easily shortened.

Detail: A fine introduction to this little-known but very scenic area. You climb 1100ft.

Map: Explorer 2 and 3 (E) or Pathfinder 165.

A largely open walk abounding in views. A slight detour was needed at the end of stage 33, where the right of way SE met an electric fence at the bottom. There can be muddy sections at 5 and 26.

Near Upper North Dean

1. Go SE along Water Lane, which is a little E along the main road from Studridge Lane. ⇗
2. At signpost go L to field corner. On in next field to stile.
3. On down path between houses. Go L along track and R down road.
4. At Spring Coppice Lane, go ½L over stile and up field. On over stile to far, top corner of field.
5. Here ⅓R along track 60m, then on along field edge. (Fence on your R, but soon on your L.)
6. On into wood 80m then R along path (10m past arrow on tree). Ignore faint, level path forking L.
7. Leave wood at stile. On down by fence.
8. L along road. At phone box, sharp R along track. On up fields by hedge on your R.
9. Bear L away from wood edge to stile 40m from it. Here along wide ridge by fence on your R.
10. At signpost go L with fence, then hedge, by your R.
11. On down R edge of wood.
12. At bottom go over stile. On up to double stile. On up field.
13. At gate go ½L over field, passing just R of trees.
14. Go ½R along field edge. R along lane.
15. Fork L before service garage, beside hedge on your R. At hedge gap go ⅓L, still by hedge on your R.
16. On over field towards nearest trees.
17. Over stile, L 50m to cross stile and bear R to bottom. Then up to gate.
18. Here sharp L along drive.
19. At road turn L. On over main road for 70m.
20. Here R along field edge.
21. On along road. L along Church Lane. Soon bear L past Crown Cottages. ⇗
22. Soon after vicarage, go L at footpath sign, between hedges. Over stile and on. Down valley to gate.
23. R along road.
24. 100m after farm, go R over stile for 30m then L up grass track, soon with hedge on your R.
25. At wood, ignore stile on L. Keep on over next stile.
26. Out of wood. Follow hedge on your R as it bears R to stile and (further on) to track. Down track. (If muddy use field on L when track starts descent.)

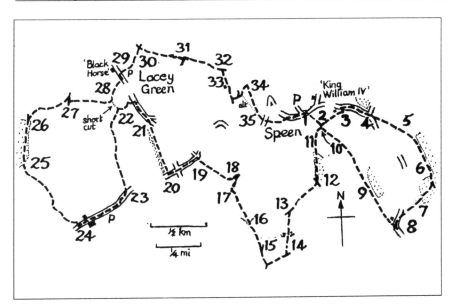

27. At bottom go sharp R 30m, sharp L down bank and straight up field. On over next field 100m to gate.

28. Along drive. L along lane. L along road 50m.

29. R along Kiln Lane.

30. Where it narrows at a mini cross-tracks, turn R. Keep on with hedge on your R.

31. R over stile 30m before gate ahead, and L to track. L along track, at once turning R.

32. When concrete track ends, go through gate on R and along top field edge.

33. Go $\frac{1}{2}$R over garden and $\frac{1}{2}$L along track. L at T-junction. On along path when track U-turns. Over stile and L along field edge.

34. Over stile and R by electric fence. Over stile and down path (fence on your R) to road.

35. Over road and along path to gate. Go up field (or if no path, go along bottom edge to stile on R and L up path). Over stile and small field to stile. Up road.

Variations

Shorter walk East (5½ miles, 9km, 750ft): Follow 1 to 21, then carry on along lane. Go L along road 50m and follow 29 to 35.

Shorter walk West (5½ miles, 9km, 800ft): Follow 1, then at signpost go R beside hedge. Follow 11 to 35.

Much shorter walk (4 miles, 6km, 450ft): Follow 1, then at signpost go R beside hedge. Follow 11 to 21, then carry on along lane. Go L along road 50m and follow 29 to 35.

Chiltern Buildings

Some timber-framed houses (15th century and on) still survive, though the framing has often been covered over. Originally the frame carried the whole load of the roof. The wall gaps were often filled with wattle and daub, later replaced by brick panels. Many brick and flint buildings can be seen – flint and clay (for bricks) were the only local building materials available in quantity. The Chiltern Open Air Museum is an excellent place to see past buildings, ranging from an Iron Age dwelling (reconstruction) to a not-so-ancient prefab. It is located in Newlands Park, Gorelands Lane, Chalfont St Giles. Telephone 01494 871 117 for opening times and charges.

Old coaching inns, often with arched entrances and cobbled yards, can be seen in the small towns such as Old Amersham, Old Beaconsfield and West Wycombe.

If you see pieces of mushroom-shaped stonework they may be staddle-stones. In the past, grain-storing barns were built resting on these to prevent rats getting in.

24. From The Pink and Lily to Pyrtle Spring

Starting Point: Lay-by near The Pink and Lily (827 019).

Access: Go N from High Wycombe on the A4128, but go straight on at roundabout and soon L uphill through Naphill. After Lacey Green, go R at crossroads and along Pink Road for 1 mile.

Distance: 4½ miles (7km).

Detail: A pleasant walk, mainly in gently hilly, open fields, with one steep, shady climb at stage 11. You climb 550ft.

Map: Explorer 2 or Pathfinder 165.

The windmill, which once stood in Chesham, is thought to be the oldest of its type in the country (1650). Restored by the Chiltern Society, it is sometimes open e.g. summer Sunday afternoons. The Pink and Lily was a favourite inn of Rupert Brooke. There may be a short muddy stretch at stage 2.

The Lacey Green windmill

1. Go back to the inn and R (SE) along lane.
2. R up track just before house. Soon ⅔R over stile and field.
3. Over stile and field to gap near pylon.
4. On over stiles (fence on your L). Leave fence to go down and up field to stile 100m R of field corner.
5. Here keep on, later with hedge and windmill on your R. Sharp R along Pink Road.
6. After a stretch of houses on your R, go sharp L over stile and down field to stile R of pole. On to and over next stile and L by hedge on your L. Bear R down to road.
7. R along road to junction. Here go on over fields, with hedge on your R after second stile.
8. Keep on when hedge goes ½R. At a crossing hedge keep on, with fence on your L.
9. At small wood, R along field path. L along track.
10. R along lane. At second R bend go on up field to stile 50m L of reservoir fence.
11. In wood ignore steps on your R. Later on along track, R along road.

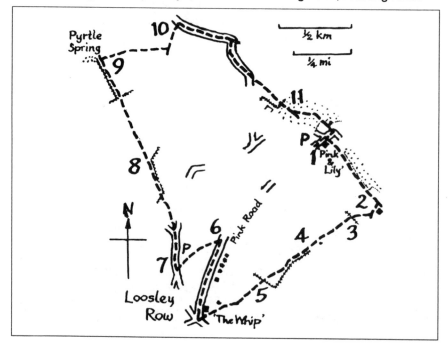

25. South-East of Speen

Starting Point: Picnic site, Hampden Road (866 991).

Access: Go N from High Wycombe on the A4128, but keep on at roundabout, along the valley. At Harrow Inn fork R along Warrendene Road and go on at crossroads to the site on your R.

Distance: 8 miles (13km). Easily shortened.

Detail: A second chance to explore this lovely area. You climb 1300ft.

Map: Explorer 2 and 3 (E) or Pathfinder 165.

Six ups and downs make this a walk of ever-changing views, with some short sections of fine beech woods. Usually pretty free of mud.

The view from high above Harrow Inn

1. From car park go L along road and soon R up field edge.
2. On over stile near top. Bear L along field edge to its corner.
3. Here go L to drive and R along it, at once forking along the L of two drives.
4. 100m after drive bends R, turn ½L at stile and go down to field corner.
5. Over road and up into wood.
6. Ignore path on L just inside wood. Soon take L fork along path, soon parallel to wood edge. Later follow arrows. ⇗
7. After path bears R near wood end, go L at path junction and 20m to stile at wood edge. Down ridge (SSE), past two clumps of trees.
8. Over stile and ½L over field to stile.
9. Again ½L over field to stile, then on to road.
10. Here ½R up lane.
11. At wood on your L, turn R up field. On over stile.
12. R at cross path, soon going down in wood. On through houses to Harrow Inn.
13. At road go R 20m then go through gate (near postbox) and over large field towards wood.
14. Just before stile go L to road.
15. Over road and ½R up field to stile in hedge. On to stile at wood edge. Over it, L 5m, then R along path.
16. Path goes into valley and up it, soon bearing L to field. Here bear R along hedge on your R.
17. At field corner go sharp R to stile 150m L of R-hand field corner. Over stile and ⅓L along path in wood.
18. Fork ½L along larger of two paths, soon descending. Watch for R fork down to stile near wood edge.
19. On down field to stile and down lane.
20. L along road, soon R to top of field.
21. Here L over stile into wood and R up path.
22. At top go L along path near top edge of wood.
23. Leave wood at stile. Carry on just outside wood.
24. Over stile. Sharp R across wood to stile. On over field to gate 80m R of house. L through gate. R along drive to lane.
25. Here into wood. At once fork L down L edge of wood. Down field, by hedge, to lane.

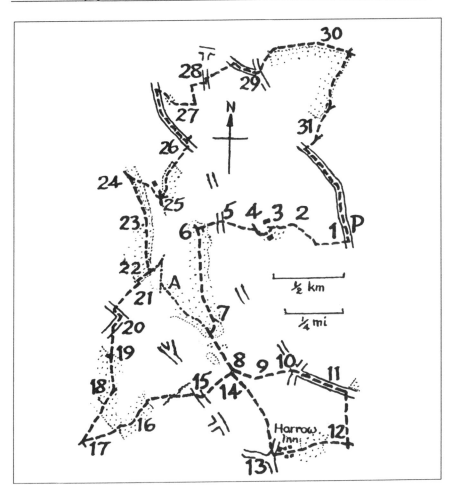

26. L along lane to second path sign on R. Here sharp R up field to stile. Over and $\frac{1}{2}$L up path in thicket to field.

27. Here $\frac{2}{3}$L over stile and up field. Go L along its top edge. Over stile and R to lane.

28. L along lane. Soon R along track. Soon through gateway and across grass to stile. Down field over stiles and down lane.

29. At junction go $\frac{1}{2}$L up field to stile and into wood. Soon out and along wood edge.

30. Down to and R over stile then along path just inside wood.

31. On down drive, L along lane.

Variation

Shorter walk (5 miles, 8km, 700ft): Follow 1 to 6,then

7. After path bears R to a junction (with stile at wood edge 20m to L) go R along path (arrowed), at first not far from wood edge.

A. Go ½R up drive 200m, then sharp L at path sign. Soon sharp R along path near top edge of wood. Now follow 23 to 31.

The Romans and Anglo-Saxons

In the two centuries before and after Christ, dramatic changes occurred in the primitive scenery as the Romans moved in, peppering the area with villas, especially to the west of Verulamium, now known as St Albans. The museum and park there are well worth a visit to see sections of brick and flint walls, hypocaust, amphitheatre, mosaics, decorated wall-plaster panels, pottery, jewellery, etc. Note also the medieval cathedral. The surrounding villas were probably farmsteads, which were abandoned (though some were later reoccupied) by AD400, when the Romans left Britain to try and cope with their Empire problems. They left a legacy of well-engineered roads, including Watling Street (A5) and Akerman Street (A41). They probably upgraded the Lower Icknield Way (now partly the B4009). After the Romans left, their system remained for a short while, together with a literate Christian culture. Then the Anglo-Saxons came to upset the situation, agriculture reverted to a more primitive level and a new language was introduced. By AD1000, the villages, farms, manors, woods, lanes and boundaries had taken on a pattern not greatly different from today.

26. The Hampdens: A Short Stroll

Starting Point: Lay-by by bottom of road to Little Hampden (863 024).

Access: Take the road WNW from Great Missenden. After 2 miles (3.5km), stop on L opposite the turning to Little Hampden.

Distance: $3\frac{1}{2}$ miles (5km).

Detail: A walk of gentle climbs in open country. You climb 400ft.

Map: Explorer 2 or Pathfinder 165.

There are plenty of rural views and short stretches of woodland to enjoy. For points of interest reached by going R after the second stile in stage 6, see the next walk.

Great Hampden church

1. Keep on (W) along road to wood end and go R with hedge on your L.

2. At corner of field on your L go through gap, now a hedge on your R.

3. Go L along crossing path into wood. Ignore path along wood edge on your R; follow arrows on path a little inside wood. At T-junction turn L. Follow main path shown by arrows.

4. Down field by hedge on your R.

5. Over road and up field by hedge on your L.

6. Over road and $\frac{1}{2}$L up field to stile in fence. Here on to stile just L of house, and L along road.

7. On over crossroads. At bend ignore first path sign; go along track at second sign just after bend. Soon ignore track forking L.

8. . Over field beside poles. At stile $\frac{1}{2}$R 30m, $\frac{1}{2}$L by fence on your L.

9. Through gap and $\frac{1}{3}$L to road. At John Hampden monument go $\frac{1}{2}$R down field to stile.

10. Over stile and on along wood edge. Go L along crossing path.

11. Over stile. Cross open strip and on in wood, ignoring R fork.

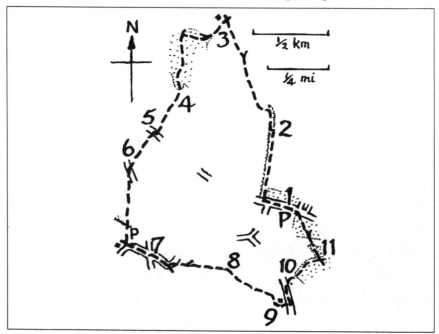

27. The Hampdens: A Longer Loop

Starting Point: Cockshoots Wood car park (872 042).

Access: Go SW along Cobblershill Lane, a turning off the A413, 2 miles (3km) S of Wendover, to the woodland car park.

Distance: 7 miles (11km). Can be shortened.

Detail: A gentler walk away from the popular Coombe Hill, still with plenty of views mingled with attractive woodland. You climb 800ft.

Map: Explorer 2 or Pathfinder 165.

The lovely Hampden valley runs from Great Missenden to Chequers. Follow the route carefully in the woods. If you are prone to getting lost, try another walk. The Hampden family were here before the Normans came. John Hampden the 'Patriot' (1594-1643) was remembered long after his death for his wisdom in political matters and for his stand in refusing to pay a certain tax. King Charles had tried to levy ship money without the consent of Parliament. What's more, he used the money for himself, not for shipbuilding. As a result of his refusal to pay, John was sued and at first lost the case, though later the judgement was cancelled.

Hampden House (now a school) was built in the 14th century, but mainly rebuilt 300 years later. The medieval church contains Hampden monuments. Beyond the church is a section of the Iron Age Grim's Ditch, perhaps a tribal boundary marker. The tiny church at Little Hampden has a unique, two-storeyed, 15th-century porch, wall paintings (including the earliest St Christopher in England), a 12th-century sculpture and pre-Reformation altar. Near it is Manor Farm, dating from the 16th century. There may be short, muddy sections e.g. at 4 and 15.

1. In the car park, go up path at right angles to the lane. Ignore smaller, level path forking L.

2. At a 6-way junction, go on along path (not track), soon along edge of your wood (on your L).

3. Cross track and bear L. After 50m ignore L fork and follow yellow arrows to wood edge.

4. Go R along track, then L along road.

5. After road bends to R, turn L along track for 50m. Then R along field edge.

6. On in wood. On down field edge (hedge on your R).

7. Through gap near field corner and $\frac{1}{3}$L down field to road.

8. On up lane. Watch for footpath sign and go R. Path goes along bottom edge of fields to wood.

9. On in wood. Path goes gently down, soon crossing a path.

10. At path junction turn L. After 120m go R along crossing path. At path junction, go sharp R to stile.

11. Over field towards farm. On over lane and along by fence on your R. At field corner go $\frac{1}{2}$R for 30m then $\frac{1}{2}$L (fence on your R at first).

12. Follow path in wood.

13. L along road. On over crossroads. Soon on along drive where road bends L.

14. Just past buildings, go through gate, and at once $\frac{2}{3}$R over stile and field.

15. On into wood. Out of wood and down field to corner.

16. Over road and along track in trees.

17. Bear R through gap and $\frac{1}{3}$R up field to small hedge gap. Up in wood. On over field.

18. $\frac{1}{2}$L at path junction to reach gap in tall hedge, 50m L of the L end of low hedge. Go on to road and R along it.

19. Go L opposite church. Follow hedge on your L down field and up.

20. At wood, go $\frac{1}{2}$L up path. ➘

21. Near top, at stiles, turn L along level path. Path stays roughly 80m from top of wood, with fairly steep ground on your L.

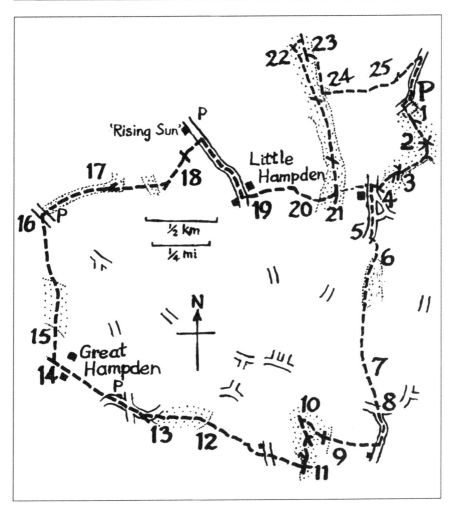

22. After going on over two crossing paths, watch for junction arrow on tree. Just before this go R along faint path. Soon R 100m along clear path, then $\frac{2}{3}$L at arrow to wood edge.

23. Over stile and R along field edge.

24. Over stile and L down fields with hedge on your L.

25. 150m before bottom, where hedge on L joins yours, go L over track and $\frac{1}{2}$R to stiles and R along lane.

The unique porch of Little Hampden church

Variation

Shorter walk (5½ miles, 8.5km, 650ft): Park at the end of the road to Little Hampden (857 040). Walk back along the road. Follow 19 to 20, then go on, soon out of wood and over field past farm. R along road. Follow 5 to 18.

28. Whiteleaf Hill

Starting Point: Car park near Pulpit Hill (833 046).

Access: Leave the A4010 at Askett roundabout (NE of Princes Risborough). After 1¼ miles (2km), use car park on your L.

Distance: 6½ miles (10km). Can be shortened.

Detail: A fine walk featuring beech woods and open downland views. You climb 850ft.

Map: Explorer 2 or Pathfinder 165.

The climax is the climb to Whiteleaf Hill, with views along the escarpment, a long barrow on the summit and a large, 18th-century chalk cross just below. Near the end, a nature reserve near Pulpit Hill is also splendid with its orchids and other chalk flora. It may be muddy at stages 9 and 23.

Grangelands nature reserve near Pulpit Hill

1. Turn L (E) out of car park, go along road and soon go R down path.

2. At small dip go L up path to stile. On by hedge (on your R).

3. At wood corner, go R along its edge.

4. At field corner, go L along next field edge (wood on your R) to farm. On down drive.

5. At bottom, go R up track (50m before you get to field).

6. While track is rising, fork ½R along arrowed path near wood edge.

7. R at path junction, so leaving wood 50m later (hedge on your R). ⮑

8. At drive turn L through iron gate then over field (hedge on your L at first) to gate.

9. L along road. At wood on R, turn R along path just outside wood.

10. At field corner turn L along track in wood (fence on your L).

11. Turn R along crossing path (arrows on tree), first in pines, then down in beeches.

12. On over fields to road. On along road.

13. R along Upper Icknield Way.

14. At fork, go R up field by fence on your R to wood edge.

15. On up path with steps. (Ignore side paths.) Over stile and on up field between bushes.

16. Near stile by road turn L, soon a fence near your R. Go up road.

17. Soon L up bank to car park. At once L. At end of car park, go on along path bearing R and ½R along track (fence on your R at first) to hilltop clearing.

18. Here go ½L gently down path.

19. Ignore L turn. Go down through gate. Bear R along fence.

20. Down lane. Turn R past front of pavilion to gate. On down golf course.

21. Through gap in tall hedges and along path to road.

22. L down road 80m and ½R along path (later with track on your L). Through gate into reserve and fork ⅓R up path. Aim for L-hand side of wooded hill.

23. At top of field, turn R along edge, passing gates. Then ½L over tree roots to stile and on along main track.

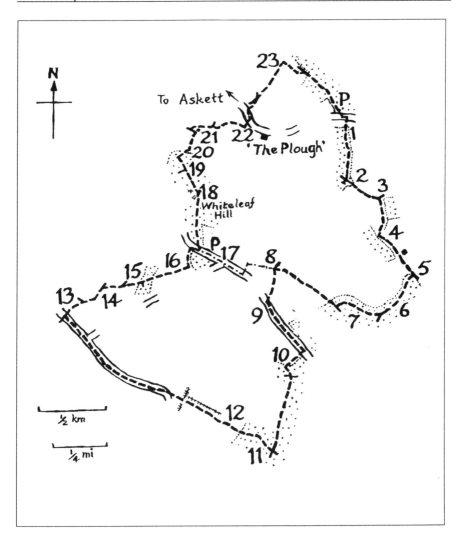

Variation

Shorter walk (4 miles, 6km, 500ft): Follow 1 to 7, then go on along drive, R along road. Enter car park and follow 17 (except the first sentence) to 23.

Chiltern Churches

There are many almost unspoilt medieval churches in this area. Outside they have flint-faced walls, as there is no other local building material. Bricks made from local clay were used in the 14th century, for example, for Stonor chapel (walks 7 and 8).

In the following lists, the numbers in brackets refer to walks near the churches mentioned. Norman churches may be seen at Fingest (5 and 6), The Lee (32) and Radnage (16 and 17). Early English churches are at Bledlow (17) and Ivinghoe (48); Decorated at Aldbury (46) and Great Missenden (32); and Perpendicular at Bradenham (18 and 20). At Little Missenden (33) there is a Saxon church, largely altered in Norman times.

The churches contain a variety of fonts, many of them Norman. The earliest were tub-shaped, as at Ibstone (4), The Lee (32) and Turville (4). A decorated cylindrical font is at Hambleden (12). The 'Aylesbury' fonts may have been made from local Tottenhoe stone and are mostly circular on a square base. These are found at Bledlow (17), Great Missenden (32) and Little Missenden (33). The font at Penn (34) is lead-lined. The one at Radnage (16 and 17) might be Saxon, but this is unlikely. Font covers are rare, there is only one dating from before the 16th century – at Ewelme (near 1), and one from the 17th century at Stokenchurch (16).

Other items of interest include brasses at Aldbury (46), Chesham Bois (38) and Penn (34); chests at Bradenham (18 and 20) and Great Gaddesden (45); and consecration crosses at Little Missenden (33), Penn (34) and Radnage (16 and 17). There are effigies at Aldbury (46), Ewelme (near 1), Hughenden (22) and Ivinghoe (48). Aldbury (46), Chesham Bois (38), Ewelme (near 1), Great Missenden (32) and Little Missenden (33) have medieval tiles, and there are photographs of unique ones at Tring (43) – the originals are in the Victoria and Albert Museum. The oak pulpit at Ibstone (4) is interesting; as is the reredos of alabaster at Hambleden (12).

Those with an interest in church architecture should see the roofs at Ewelme (near 1), Great Missenden (32), Ivinghoe (48), Little Missenden (33), Penn (34) and Radnage (16 and 17). The screens at Aldbury (46) and Ewelme and Swyncombe (1) are very attractive, while the stained glass at Bradenham (18 and 20), The Lee (32), Turville (4), West Wycombe (19, 20 and 21) is particularly impressive.

Churches in the Chilterns will also provide you with an opportunity to admire the craftsmanship of early stonemasons. Walks 26, 27 and 30 will allow you to visit the stone altar at Little Hampden, and there is a stone coffin in the churchyard at Ibstone (4). Further interesting stonework can be seen at Bledlow (17), Great Gaddesden (45) and Ivinghoe (48), all of which have stiff-leafed capitals and arcading. The doorway at Bradenham (18 and 20) is possibly Saxon, and there are tomb chests at Aldbury (46) and Chesham Bois (38). Early wall paintings are always interesting and it's worth allowing the time to view those at Little Hampden (26, 27 and 30), Little Missenden (33), Penn (34), Radnage (16 and 17) and Swyncombe (1).

29. Coombe and Whitleaf Hills

Starting Point: Lay-by at the foot of Coombe Hill (847 071).

Access: Go W from Wendover for 1 ¼ miles (2km) towards Ellesborough and park on L opposite golf club house.

Distance: 7 ½ miles (12km). Can be shortened.

Detail: A great walk between two fine hills. You climb 1250ft.

Map: Explorer 2 or Pathfinder 165.

The initial steep climb to Coombe Hill is rewarded with splendid views from the Boer War monument and the open ridge. Beautiful stretches of beech woods are met on the way to Whiteleaf Hill, where there are more views, a long barrow on the top and an 18th-century chalk cross just below. A classic return passes through a nature re-

The descent to Ellesborough

serve (with orchids and other downland flora), an area of box trees (rarely found growing wild in Britain), and Ellesborough (an unspoilt village beneath its towering church) before crossing a large field to reach the foot of Coombe Hill. The shorter walks get as near as you can to Chequers, an Elizabethan house given to the nation for the use of the prime minister.

1. At road sign 'Ellesborough' turn S off road towards Coombe Hill. Ignore L fork. Go through gate and then fork L uphill.

2. At monument, $\frac{1}{2}$R along nearly level path with shrubs on your L.

3. Bear L along fence. Soon R through gate and on along top wood edge.

4. Go R down road 100m, L along track and soon on over second stile. Along track near wood edge, R over stile and L along track.

5. Follow acorn signs (on at crossing path, L at T-junction, on at crossing path and on past junction sign about 10m R of main track).

6. R down track (acorn sign). On over crossing track and $\frac{1}{3}$R along field edge. ⮑

7. L along road past farm.

8. Just after last house, go R over field to road.

9. Here L 20m then R between fences up into strip of trees, later into wood.

10. At cross path marked by arrows, go R.

11. At junction sign turn L. Cross line of poles and later a track.

12. Turn R along road and soon L along track.

13. At small dip go R along path. Follow arrows, going $\frac{1}{2}$R down to valley bottom.

14. Here L along track to 5-way junction, and $\frac{1}{2}$L up path.

15. Go L up path on ridge. At hilltop turn R down. On down lane.

16. Turn R past front of pavilion to gate. On down golf course.

17. Go $\frac{1}{2}$L to keep by tall hedge (on your R) down to road.

18. Over road and on up path, then $\frac{1}{3}$R over field.

19. At far field corner go on 30m (fence on your R) to signpost. Here go $\frac{1}{2}$L up through gate and on. Follow yellow arrows.

20. Up to steps, stile and on. Soon $\frac{1}{2}$R up track 30m. Over stile and on (yellow arrows) to pass along top of deep valley and up to gate. ⮑

21. Here go L over stile and along by fence (on your R). On up small hill and ½R down to stile.

22. On with fence on your L to stile by gate.

23. On over drive, through wood and over field on nearly level path.

24. Down among dark box trees, over grass and down field to church.

25. Turn R along road and soon R again along track.

26. At hedge gap, go ½L across field to road.

27. Go R along road 100m, then L along track up to wood.

28. Here L along wood edge to road.

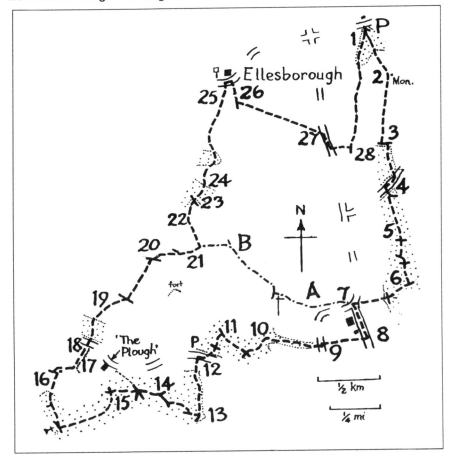

Variations

Coombe Hill (5 miles, 7.5km, 600ft): Follow 1 to 6, then on over road and field, past pole and leftish to cross drive.

A. Here on, then ⅓R over field to stile and R along track at wood edge to iron gate.

B. Go ½L over field to gate then R, along by fence kept on your R. Go down to and over stile and follow 22 to 28.

Whiteleaf Hill (4½ miles, 7km, 800ft): Park near Pulpit Hill as in walk 28. Go L out of car park along road and soon R down track. Follow 13 to 20, then at gate go ⅓R over field to gate.

B. Here go ½R to follow wood edge, keeping outside, later with fence on your L. At sign go L down field to drive.

A. Go ⅓L over drive and field, bearing R to stile. Here go ½R along lane past farm. Now follow 8 to 11 and go R along road.

Downland Flowers

The ultimate Chiltern floral experience is to visit chalk downland in early summer and to sink down amongst its tiny flowers – the fragrant thyme and exotic orchids. (Take care not to sink down on to a stemless thistle.) The plants tend to be small because of the poor soil and grazing by rabbits or sheep. Common spotted, pyramidal and fragrant orchids are often seen. Bee orchids are spectacular but less frequent. (Even the very rare lizard orchid occurs at one location.) Apart from the BBONT downland reserves, it is worth visiting Ivinghoe Beacon (47), Watlington Hill (2) and Coombe Hill (29 and 30). The latter has juniper, yew and whitebeam on its slopes, while its plateau (not chalk, but clay with flints) is heathland with gorse, broom and heather.

Other interesting flowers you may see include cowslips, clustered bell-flower, musk thistle, rock rose, yellow-wort, harebells and carline thistle.

Several beautiful gentians grow on the downs. The Chiltern gentian, with its larger than usual flowers, occurs on many of the downs but is rarely seen outside the area. In 1875 a strange gentian was found on Coombe Hill, and was misidentified. It was rediscovered in 1982 and turned out to be fringed gentian, which grows nowhere else in Britain.

Wild candytuft is often seen (e.g. Watlington Hill and Warburg reserve) but seldom met with outside the area. The pasque flower is perhaps the most beautiful of all, with large purple petals, a contrasting centre of yellow stamens and wonderfully downy leaves. As they are often removed, they have declined in numbers, though a few survive on the Ivinghoe ridge. Plans are being made to reintroduce them in certain areas.

30. Coombe Hill and Little Hampden

Starting Point: Little Hampden (857 040).

Access: Go WNW from Great Missenden for 2 miles (3.5km) and turn R to the end of the road to Little Hampden.

Distance: 7½ miles (11.5km). Can be shortened.

Detail: A different ascent of Coombe Hill combined with a visit to Hampden country. You climb 950ft.

Map: Explorer 2 or Pathfinder 165.

A fine selection of beech woods and views are met, and the route dodges the new Wendover bypass to reach a splendid ridge climb to Coombe Hill. Little Hampden Church is a little further S of point 2. See walk 27.

Morris dancing on Coombe Hill, 7am May Day Bank Holiday

1. Walk back (SE) along road.

2. At end of grass triangle, go L along track into wood. Soon fork R off main track.

3. On leaving wood, go down field with hedge on your R.

4. Up second field (hedge on your L) and on steeply up in wood.

5. L along clear, level path 80m from top edge of wood, with steep ground on your L. Stay on this path, ignore crossing path, R forks and turns.

6. When path starts to descend, fork R (20m before signpost) along path that bears R to follow fence on your L. Go L along track. ⮡

7. R along road. Soon L along path. After 100m go R at path junction.

8. L over stile. Soon R along inside wood edge. At wood end go R along field edge 70m and $\frac{2}{3}$L over field to stile (or round edge if no path).

9. Here on along drive. Just before farm go sharpish L over field for 150m, to stile in hedge. Here go on over field at about 30 degrees to hedge on your R. Later make for R-hand end of line of trees.

10. Here go on down path with hedge on your R. Over track and stile. Up field and on into wood.

11. Go $\frac{1}{2}$L across field.

12. Over stile and $\frac{1}{3}$L up field. Keep just R of shrubs. Over stile and on between fences.

13. Turn L along lane and $\frac{1}{2}$R up field at signpost.

14. On over track and up path, soon fork R. At top of rise go L up ridge path.

15. Through wood by either gate and on to monument.

16. Here go $\frac{2}{3}$L along nearly level path with shrubs on your L. ⮡

17. Bear L along fence. Soon R through gate and on along wood edge.

18. Go R down road 100m, L along track and soon on over second stile. Along track near wood edge, R over stile and L along track.

19. Follow acorn signs (on at crossing path, L at T-junction, on at crossing path and on past junction sign about 10m R of main track). ⮡

20. R down track (acorn sign). On over crossing track and $\frac{1}{3}$R along field edge.

21. L along lane. When it enters wood, turn R. Fork R along wood edge.

22. Fork $\frac{2}{3}$L up path, soon with field to your R. Through pines.

23. Follow path as it leaves wood and goes along field edge, soon with hedge on your R.

24. At field corner, go R then L, now with hedge on your L.

25. On over track into wood. Bear R along track. (If muddy use path L of track.)

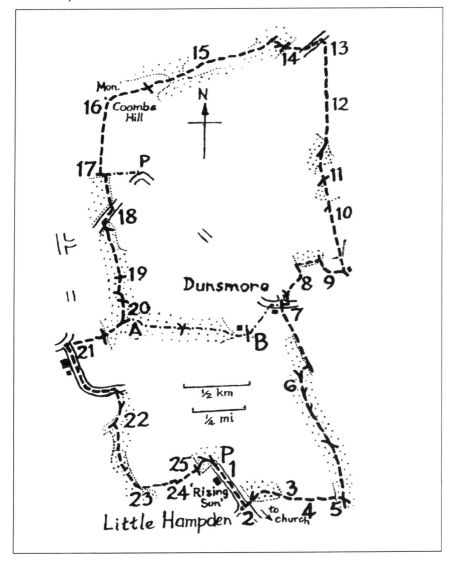

Variations

Coombe Hill (5 miles, 8km, 700ft): At the crossroads at Butler's Cross, W of Wendover, drive S, then turn L uphill to the car park at the right-angled bend (852 062). Walk through gate and take the L fork, with fence near your L. Go L through gate and on along top wood edge. Follow 18 to 19, then go sharp L up track.

A. Bear R with track along edge of clearing (on your L). On at junction.

B. At track end, go on up field over stiles. Bear $\frac{1}{3}$L to stile. On up to house.

7. At road go R, passing junction. Soon L along path 100m and R at path junction. Now follow 8 to 15 and go L beside crossing fence (at 17).

Little Hampden (4½ miles, 6.5km, 550ft): Follow 1 to 6, then L along road 80m and ½L over stile and down field. Watch for stile in fence ahead. Over and down over stiles to buildings.

B. On up track. At junction keep on along track.

A. Bear L with track near end of clearing. After descent go $\frac{1}{3}$R along field edge. Follow 21 to 25.

31. Wendover Dean

Starting Point: Lay-by on A413, S of Wendover, at 879 045.

Access: Drive S 2 miles (3.5km) from Wendover to either of two lay-bys, both near a minor turning on the E side.

Distance: 6½ miles (10km). Can be shortened.

Detail: Plenty of views on both sides of this pleasant vale. You climb 700ft.

Map: Explorer 2 or Pathfinder 165.

The East side has attractive, open fields, while the West side includes a lovely beech wood, which is omitted in the shorter walk. The track in stage 15 can be muddy.

1. Go along this minor road. At T-junction go ⅓L to stile and up field. Make for path sign L of holly tree and buildings.

2. On over track. Up field to stile halfway along the field's side. On to next stile.

3. On up open field, then ½L across it to just L of houses. L along road.

4. 50m before T-junction, go sharp L over stile and down field. Lower down there will be a hedge on your L.

5. At bottom field corner go on by hedge on your R. Soon follow hedge R.

6. Turn L down track. Soon on along lane, passing farm.

7. Up grass track between hedges. It forks near its end. Take L fork along field edge with hedge on your R.

8. Turn L, R, R round barn. L to road and R along it.

9. Just after T-junction go R along path in wood. Then down field with hedge on your R.

10. After bearing R, go L down field edges (fence or hedge on your R).

11. Go L along road and soon R along path. Go ½R up field. On over stile (R of L-hand white gate). ℞

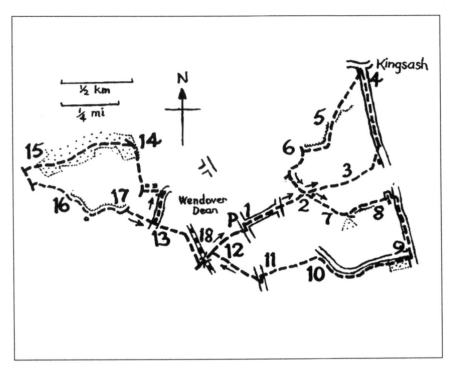

12. At far field corner go L over railway and R along field edge. Soon ½L to walk by fence on your L.

13. Go R along lane. Sharp L up the further of 2 drives. Turn R after last barn on your R.

14. Soon after entering wood, fork ½L up path. Follow arrows.

15. Over field and L along track. Soon L at track junction.

16. On over stile. Follow hedge, kept on your L. Near pond bear L through gate, still by hedge on your L.

17. When track goes through gate, go ½R over field to stile. On over lane. Later L over railway.

18. Down field to stile. Here ⅓R to next stile and L along road.

Variation

Shorter walk (4 miles, 6km, 450ft): Follow 1 to 11, then at far field corner go R and follow 18.

32. Around Great Missenden

Starting Point: The Lee (900 043).

Access: From Chesham, go NW through Chartridge and turn L through Lee Clump to The Lee. Park by the green.

Distance: $8\frac{1}{2}$ miles (13.5km). Can be shortened.

Detail: Gentle climbs on both sides of the valley, while skirting round the edge of the town. You climb 900ft.

Map: Explorer 2 or Pathfinder 165.

The Lee has a manor house and a tiny, 12th-century church which is located near to the later one. Church Farm (partly 13th century) and the churches stand within a prehistoric fort, the banks of which can be seen. A Bronze Age gold bracelet was found near The Lee in 1993. Starting on a plateau, you are soon to enjoy a valley view and an attractive ridge on the other side. Great Missenden has a coaching inn, The George, dating from 1480. The church, in a pleasant setting above the town, has a Norman font. Missenden Abbey is not an abbey, though on the site of one founded in 1133. To see the imposing figurehead mentioned on page 25, go L down the lane after stage 30. Expect some muddy patches in damp seasons.

1. Go NW along the road and L through churchyard, past both churches.
2. Over stile and L over drive. Bear slightly L to cross stile.
3. Follow fence (on your L) to wood.
4. On in wood. Turn R at its corner, now just outside wood.
5. On over road and down field (hedge on your R).
6. At pines, on down fields past end of small wood and on to road (now hedge on your R).
7. L along road. R up shady track. On up path where track narrows.
8. At top go L along path then L along path 20m after reaching wood.
9. On emerging, carry on down edge of field.

10. Where hedge goes ½R keep on. Soon down steps and on.

11. Over stile and across next field to bridge. ↘

12. Here go R, aiming just R of line of houses.

13. At road go L, then soon R up field edge (hedge on your L).

14. On reaching road, bear L along it.

15. Over main road and ½R along path. Soon on along larger path.

16. Near wood edge, go sharp L down valley track.

17. Just before wood ends, go R up path by its edge.

18. At top wood corner, ½L along track (near house). Soon ½L down lane.

19. Just before main road, turn R over grass (hedge on your L).

20. After passing school, and just after two trees on your R, turn L over road and on along track to field. Go ½L up field to bridge and over it.

21. On past church, up R fork of two drives. Where drive bears L, go on up path to road.

22. On over road, and up road for 80m. Then fork L along track. Soon ignore R fork. When track bears R, go on through small gate between fence and wall.

23. On in wood. At wood end, L down field (hedge on your L) to road.

24. Over road and on down road 30m to stile. Here go R (hedge on your L).

25. Go R over stile (30m past tunnel) and over road. Then go ½L up fields over stile, low wire, stile in hedge and stile.

26. Bear R, at first near hedge on your R. Then on up field to stile. Over stile, ⅓L to hedge gap and on by hedge on your L.

27. 150m before water tower, go L over stile and R by hedge.

28. Go R along road 100m, then sharp L over field to stile in hedge. Here over stiles and ⅓R to field corner.

29. Here on to stile by pole at field corner. On over field to gate in far corner.

30. On along shady track.

31. Go R 20m along lane and turn L.

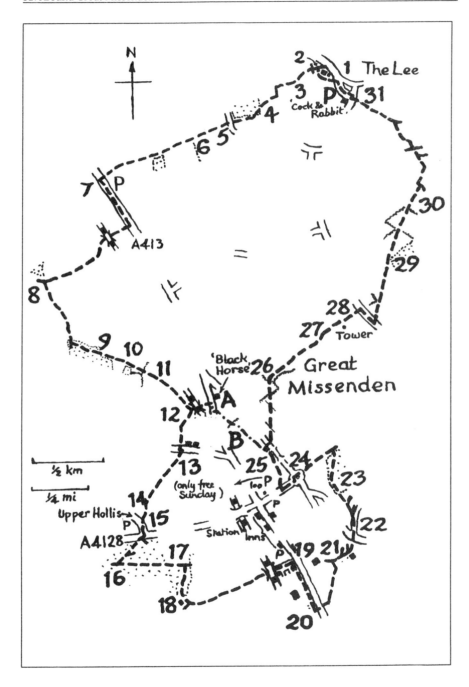

The Lee village green

Variation

North of Great Missenden (6 miles, 9km, 500ft): Follow 1 to 11, then go ½L under railway and on to road.

A. R along road 50m, L into field and at once R to stile in hedge.

B. On over next field to far L corner. Cross road and follow second sentence of stage 25 and on.

33. Little Missenden

Starting Point: Little Missenden Church (921 990).

Access: Turn off the A413 W of Amersham. Park near the church.

Distance: 8 miles (12.5km). Can be shortened.

Detail: An easy and enjoyable walk from an unspoilt village. You climb 650ft.

Map: Explorer 2 and 3 (E) or Pathfinder 165.

The village has some lovely houses dating from the 16th century. The church is special. It was Saxon, but then enlarged by the Normans. Features include a blocked Saxon window, Norman font, 15th-century porch and remarkable 13th-century wall paintings. Another feature of this valley is the River Misbourne, unusual in chalk country. However, it has a habit of disappearing for long periods. Mud may be found in places e.g. stages 6 and 14.

Little Missenden church

1. Go R over stile just L of church and on along field edge.

2. On over road, up field and over bridge.

3. On 10m, and ½L up main track, parallel with and near R edge of wood.

4. Go out of wood and on along field edge.

5. R along road 10m and L along path, soon crossing a wider one. (If muddy, use road.)

6. Near houses go R along track. Soon follow yellow arrows across lawn and on.

7. On over field to pass The Plough. Turn R along Brays Lane.

8. On down Chalk Lane 100m, L over stile into wood 20m, and then ½R down path.

9. At wood edge go over two stiles and field to bridge (or use path between fences).

10. Over bridge and R. At stile go L along field edge to road.

11. Here go R 50m, then L over main road and on down lane.

12. After crossing river, go L along track.

13. Just after a crossing track, go R through gate. Follow fence uphill.

14. Well after path levels, go R over stile at small wood and L along track. (If muddy, path in wood avoids some of it.)

15. At buildings, go along lane 80m, and R along field edge to stile in hedge gap.

16. Over stile and ½R over field to stile. On by hedge to road.

17. Here ½L for 20m, then ½R along field edge.

18. Go ⅓R down to wood corner, through wood and on up to road.

19. Go R along road (bearing R). Just past junction go L along enclosed path. Soon go R along crossing path. Pass just L of garages.

20. Over road and along path almost opposite. Over stile and on to far L corner of field, passing just R of jutting out hedge corner.

21. Over stile and along by hedge (on your L) to stile.

22. Here, on over drive and along the R of two parallel paths.

23. Where the two paths join, go ½R down track.

24. Sharp R along drive, then ⅓R by fence on your R, down ridge.

25. Over stile and down by hedge (on your L) until it turns L. Then on up to ridge path.

26. R down this path. Through hedge gap and $\frac{1}{3}$L over field, soon with hedge on your L.

27. Over track and on to stile just L of houses. On along road.

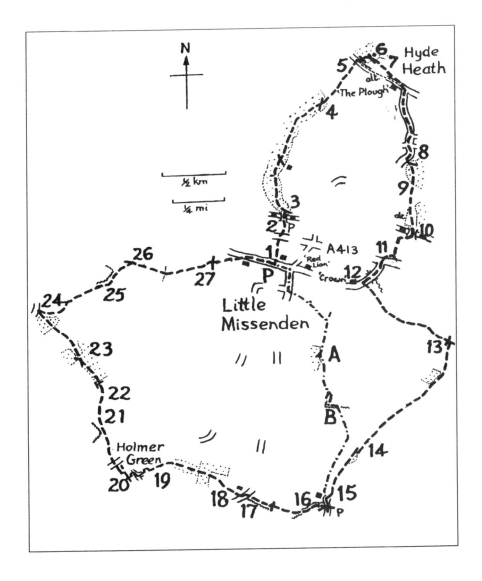

Variation

Shorter walk (5 miles, 7.5km, 450ft): At church go E along road 50m and R along road to junction. Go ½L over field and past tree to track then ½R up it.

A.   Ignore path into wood. As path turns ½R go L over stile, R beside hedge and soon L at field corner (still hedge on your R).

B.   At gap go ½R to far field corner and ½R (by hedge on your L) to gate and stile. Over stile on L and continue beside track. Go back R over stile and L. Follow 15 to 27.

Transport in the Chilterns

At first there were only packhorse routes (e.g. Collier's Lane between Stokenchurch and Radnage). These were unable to cope with the increased transport of goods and people by carts and coaches in the 17th century. From 1700, turnpike trusts were set up to maintain the major routes, and these were financed by tolls collected en route. Numerous routes crossed the Chilterns, mostly radiating out from London. Tollhouses may still be seen at Bix on the A4130 near Henley and in the Chiltern Open Air Museum.

Canals appeared around 1800. One – the Grand Junction Canal – climbed to 430ft at Tring. It had many leakage problems, and reservoirs were built near Tring in an attempt to replenish them. Its route through the Chilterns was from near Watford through Berkhamstead to Tring. Here it divided into three routes to reach Aylesbury, Birmingham and Wendover. One important consequence was the drop in coal prices, which became cheaper than wood, at least near the wharves. The Duke of Bridgewater was a pioneer of canal building, although he was not involved with the Grand Junction Canal. His statue on a tall column looks down on Aldbury and this canal.

The first proposed rail route through Amersham and the Wendover Gap was rejected as a result of protests by landowners and those profiting from road and canal transport. (However, a line did follow that route in 1892.) Instead, a route from Euston, through Berkhamstead and Tring, was built in 1839. Two other routes followed: from High Wycombe to Princes Risborough, and through Luton and Dunstable. The line near Saunderton has an interesting feature near 480 010: the up and down lines leave each other for a while so that the up line has a smaller gradient.

34. South from Penn

Starting Point: Near phone box in Penn (908 930).

Access: Going N from High Wycombe on the A404, turn R along the B474. After a Z-bend and at a gentle curve L in Penn, go R along lane to just past phone box.

Distance: 7½ miles (12km). Can be shortened.

Detail: Pleasant, rolling hills sandwiched between High Wycombe and Beaconsfield. You climb 750ft.

Map: Explorer 3 (E) or Pathfinder 175.

After a brief visit N of Penn you move S to reach a scenic ridge. You pay for this in M40 traffic noise before turning back to a panoramic view from the top edge of a golf course. Penn Church has items of interest: Norman font, consecration crosses and a rare 'Doom' wall painting. At times there may be short stretches of mud at stages 2, 16, 23 and A.

The Crown, Penn

1. Go back past phone box. Soon go R along track 30m and fork ½L. On down field.
2. At stile bear R along track. Soon ½L up track.
3. L along road. Soon R, between fences at first.
4. Just after farm, go R along path (hedge on your L).
5. 80m after meeting wood on your L, go R down and up path.
6. On through wood. On over stile. R along road, soon L along lane.
7. Go L along path just before vicarage. R along drive.
8. When drive goes L, keep on along wood edge. Watch for R fork to stile at wood edge.
9. Here go R to field corner and sharp L over field, soon by fence on your R.
10. By houses, go R up track, sharp L along lane, and R up path, passing about 100m R of barn.
11. Down to stile near double pole. On down by hedge on your R.
12. Go into wood and ½L along path. On over two fields.
13. R along track, then on over stile on L, and L along lane.
14. When lane turns L, keep on over stile and between hedge and fence.
15. R along A40. At top of rise, make a U-turn R and soon L up path between fence and hedge. On up ridge (fence on your L).
16. Cross railway 10m R of fence, and turn L. R over stile and ½L over field to cross next stile.
17. Here R along in fields (fence on your R). On over field to stile. (If muddy, go back over stile to walk with fence on your L. Follow fence as it bends R and L to reach stage 18.)
18. Over stile, on 50m and L along track between hedges.
19. Just before the way ahead starts to drop, go R with track (high bank on your R). At drive, go up bank by gate to stile then ½R over field to stile under trees.
20. Here go ½R along edge of golf course. On into wood.
21. Leave wood and go sharp L along track. Soon fork L down track which bears R. Soon fork R into trees, soon go down L 30m and R along track on edge of course.
22. On when trees on your R end. 80m before farm, go L, and soon R on path with fence on your R.
23. Turn R at golf course corner. Bear L along lane.

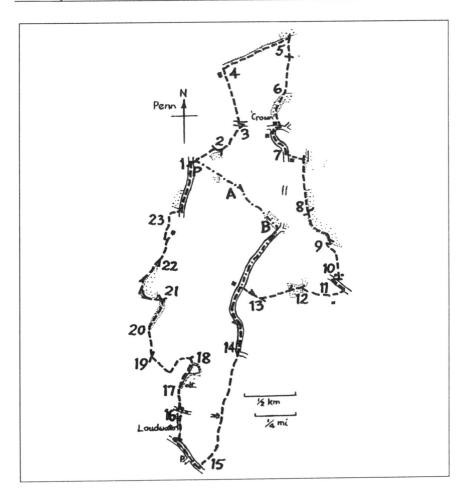

Variation

Shorter walk (5 miles, 7.5km, 450ft):

1. Go back past phone box. Soon go R along track 30m and fork R between lines of shrubs. On over fields.

A. At bottom, cross stile and go down path. On in wood.

B. 50m before gate, fork R along path and R along lane. Follow 14 to 23.

35. South from Amersham Old Town

Starting Point: At a turning off the A355 (960 969).

Access: The quiet turning is 50m S of the bypass roundabout, which is 200m S of the roundabout by Tesco's where the A413 and A355 join.

Distance: 7½ miles (11.5km). Can be shortened.

Detail: Gentle climbs, wide views and an interesting town. You climb 700ft.

Map: Explorer 3 (E) or Pathfinder 165 and 175.

The walk starts with a splendid climb out of the Misbourne valley, and ends on a wide, open ridge. Luckings and Bowers Farms date from the 17th century. The beautiful market town has many 16th-century buildings lining its wide main street. These include the Market Hall (with open arcade), the original grammar school, almshouses and several coaching inns. Parts of the church are 12th century and there are 15th-century brasses and memorials inside. There is a pleasant, 18th-century Baptist chapel.

1. 50 m along the side road, go R along path, over bridge, R to road, and L down to the roundabout near Tesco's.
2. Here go R 50m, then R 10m, and L along track under road to gate.
3. Here go ⅓R up fields to the L-hand corner of wood.
4. Into wood at stile. On out of wood towards distant pylon.
5. At hedge corner go on over field.
6. Follow hedge (kept on your R) to stile 50m before wood.
7. Go R over stile and L to fence corner near far end of wood.
8. Here go ½R (S) over field, under cables, to stile in hedge.
9. ½L over stile and down fields (soon hedge on your R). Over stile just L of barns.
10. R along road. Soon L up track (hedge on your R). Fork R.

11. After passing house, track goes L. Here sharp R over stile and along path.

12. Over stile and on over field to stile.

13. On down and up field to fence corner.

14. On with fence on your R. On over lane (hedge on your L).

15. At once in next field, go L over stile and R by hedge on your R.

16. In next field, keep on when hedge bends R. On over stile (hedge on your R).

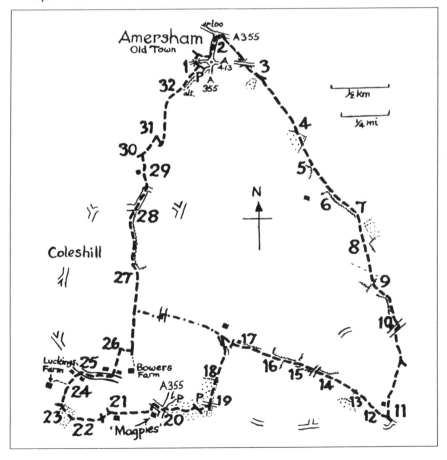

17. Just after passing house, go on over small field. Turn sharp L (near stile) along field edge and past a second stile. Cross third stile and go L to follow field edge.

18. On along track in wood to road.

19. Over road. Follow path $\frac{1}{2}$R 70m to track and R down it. It bears L. Soon fork L (car park on your R). Ignore crossing and side paths.

20. At road, go L 20m and R 100m along side road. Then go L up track.

21. At farm, leave track and go on over stile, over cross track and on along field edge (hedge on your R).

22. On in wood (bearing slightly R) to far edge.

23. On out of wood 30m, then R through iron gate (fence on your L).

24. Over stile, $\frac{1}{3}$R over field to stile (between houses) and out to road.

25. R along road. L just before second house on L. Soon along edge of two fields (hedge on your L).

26. At second field's end, go R 100m then L over open fields.

27. Over stile and along by hedge on your R to road.

28. Here go on until road goes R, then go $\frac{1}{2}$L down path.

29. At field, bear L along its edge. After slight rise you reach a bank which separates two fields.

30. Go R along bottom of bank.

31. At bank end, go sharp R to valley bottom, up bank and L along path.

32. On with hedge on your R. At field corner, go R (or L to continue walk over bridge).

Variation

Shorter walk (5$\frac{1}{2}$ miles, 9km, 550ft): Follow 1 to 16, then, after passing house, go on over stiles.

A. After rough area, go R through gap and L along field edge (hedge on your L).

B. At road go a short way L, then R down bank and up field. At hedge gap, go R along open path. Follow 27 to 32.

36. Burnham Beeches and Egypt Woods

Starting Point: Near The Yew Tree (957 868), N of Egypt.

Access: The inn is just off the A355, 1½ miles (2.5km) S of the M40, junction 2.

Distance: 4½ miles (7km).

Detail: An easy stroll in a area noted for its beauty. You climb 250ft.

Map: Explorer 3 (E) or Pathfinder 175.

This is an area of ancient natural woodland – mainly pollarded beech and oak. Lovely in winter, spring and especially autumn. Hartley (or Hardicanute's) Court was a 12th-century homestead protected by surrounding banks and ditches. In places I have used quiet roads where the network of paths is hard to follow.

Typical beechwoods near Hartley Court

1. Go SE along the lane beside the inn. Later turn R over stile into wood.

2. Cross road and on between fences. L along lane. Soon use path on your R beside road.

3. Fork R along Dukes Drive. Later go R along McAuliffe Drive.

4. Note plaque 10m R of drive and moat beyond. Soon bear R along track at four-way junction.

5. Over lane and ½R along path. Later ignore turning on your R.

6. Over field and along wood edge. Go R along lane and R at each of the next two lane junctions.

7. On along track when lane turns R. Into wood along path nearest its edge.

8. Go into wood at dip. Ignore crossing path.

9. At gate keep on to lane, R along it and on over road.

10. At farm, curve R up field to single tree, and on (hedge on your L).

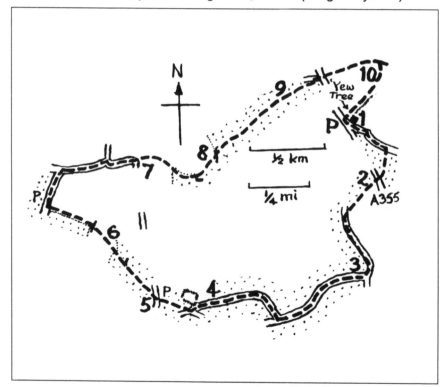

37. Ley Hill to Latimer

Starting Point: The Swan at Leyhill Common (990 019).

Access: From Chesham, take the B4505 to the top of the hill and take the second turn off the roundabout. At the common take the R of the triple fork for 50m.

Distance: 7½ miles (12km). Can be shortened.

Detail: A largely open walk with plenty of views. You climb 850ft.

Map: Explorer 2 and 3 (E) (show part of walk) or Pathfinder 165 and 166.

A good, open ridge is walked before reaching Latimer, where there was once a Roman villa. After glimpses of the River Chess, medieval Blackwell Farm, and a pleasant garden, there is a hilly return with good views, though these are sometimes obscured by the hedges of

Latimer village

the old lanes. These lanes are unsurfaced and sometimes muddy e.g. at 13. When paths are bad, try the splendid, clockwise 2-mile road circuit, starting at point A and going R at each junction.

1. Go over golf course (SE) between two roads. L along road, R at T-junction.

2. When road bends ½R, turn L on track which bears L then R, and then goes straight along a broad ridge.

3. Go R along road and L up into wood at signpost.

4. At top of wood, turn R along track inside wood. At fork, go down (R).

5. On leaving wood, go through gate, down track and L along road.

6. At green triangle, turn ½R. After 50m, go R up path between railings. On over field and through gate to road.

7. R along road and past L bend. Where road bends R, go on over stile and field, then L 30m and R along wood edge.

8. At far field corner, go down into wood. On leaving wood, go ½R along field edge.

9. Through gate and along field edges (hedge on your L). Pass just L of barns.

10. On along road 50m, then R along drive for 20m and L past flower beds. On through gate, first by wall, then fence.

11. As fence bears L, keep on along path.

12. Over stile at end of field. On along bank to stile.

13. Go R up enclosed track (soon ignore gate into field on R). (If muddy, try going R along road 80m and R up track to point 15.)

14. At fork, keep on along field edge between hedge and fence. L along track.

15. At bottom, where track bends L, go on 50m over field, over track and on up field edges (hedge on your R).

16. At open field, go on to stile 70m R of farm and R along track.

17. At bottom, go R for 20m, then L up by field edge. At top field corner go ⅓R along next field edge.

18. At field corner, go over stile and on to stile just L of inn.

19. Do **not** climb stile, but go L 150m down field edge to stile.

20. Here, cross road and go just into drive. Then over stile on the R, and diagonally over field to double stile. On over next field to stile into wood.

21. On in wood 10m, go ½R 10m and bear L to keep 20m from wood edge for a while.

22. Just after path reaches edge at a fence right angle, turn R along path. Turn L at post and soon L along larger path.

23. On over field to corner stile. On between fences.

24. Go R, L, and R along rough roads.

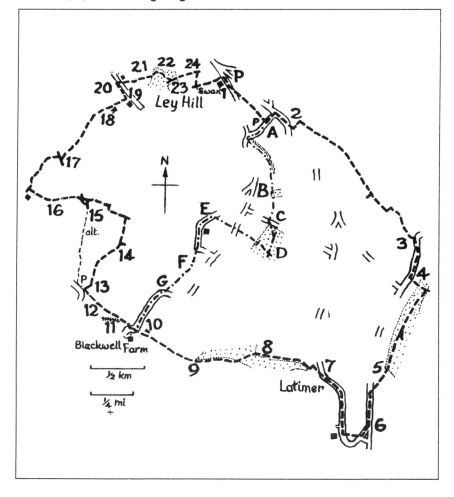

Variation

South from Ley Hill (5 miles, 8km, 800ft): Go over golf course (SE) between two roads.

A. R along road. At bottom, go L along by wood then fence on your L.

B. At field corner go over two stiles, on by wood edge and soon over field (hedge on your R).

C. Go L along road 20m, $\frac{1}{2}$R along path in wood and R along track.

D. Turn R along crossing track. On over field, road and on by fence.

E. Go L along road passing farm. On over field when road goes L.

F. Over stile in hedge and $\frac{1}{3}$R down to corner stile.

G. On down road. At footpath sign on L, follow 10 to 24.

38. North from Chesham Bois

Starting Point: Chesham Bois (958 994).

Access: From Chesham, go S on the A416 about 1 mile and park in Bois Avenue, a R turn just after the A416 bends L.

Distance: 7 miles (11km). Can be shortened.

Detail: A beech wood, an old town and plenty of views. You climb 950ft.

Map: Explorer 2 and 3 (E) or Pathfinder 165.

After a good ridge approach you pass through some charming old parts of Chesham, with some buildings dating from the 17th century. A detour L along the main road to Church Street, just beyond the roundabout, is rewarding. The church dates from the 12th century, including part of a Norman window. It has traces of a large wall

The River Chess

painting. The River Chess (not much more than a stream, if it has not dried up) is crossed twice, and medieval Blackwell Farm seen. Around the town there is a remarkable extent of unspoilt hillside. A beautiful 13th-century church is passed before the final, glorious beech wood. There may be one or two muddy patches. The worst can be bypassed at stage 14.

1. At bend in the road go along Mayhall Lane. Fork L at lane end.
2. Just before farm go R. Soon over two stiles and on (hedge on your L).
3. On in next fields. (Hedge now on R.) On down fields when hedge goes R.
4. Through gate at flat bottom of field and ½L to houses.
5. L along road, then L twice to reach larger road. R down it to Chesham.
6. Cross main road and go R 20m, then L. Soon fork R up to steps. On over railway, go R 50m, sharp L 50m and R uphill.
7. At open field, go on up to stile.
8. Over stile and L along hedge (on your L). R at corner for 100m.
9. L across field to stile. On over farm track, now by hedge (on your L).
10. When hedge turns L, go ⅓R over field. Aim just R of distant, tall mast to reach stile in hedge.
11. Over stile and down to bottom. On up field edge (fence on your L).
12. At top field corner go R down to bottom then R 20m and L up track. ↳
13. 70m before farm, go L over stile and field to second stile. On down fields.
14. On over track and 50m of field. On up shady track. (If muddy, go R along track and L 80m along road to point 16.)
15. At top, go R between fence and hedge. On down shady track.
16. Just before road, go L over stile and along bank to stile.
17. Go ⅓L over next field. Along drive, R to lane and R along it.
18. Over road and on along path to field. On by fence and under railway.
19. On in wood. Keep on main track. It later narrows. On along road 200m.
20. At T-junction, go on along footpath. Cross road it reaches, climb bank and turn R along path.
21. ½L over stile and field. Over second stile and L along stony lane. Bear R after passing church.

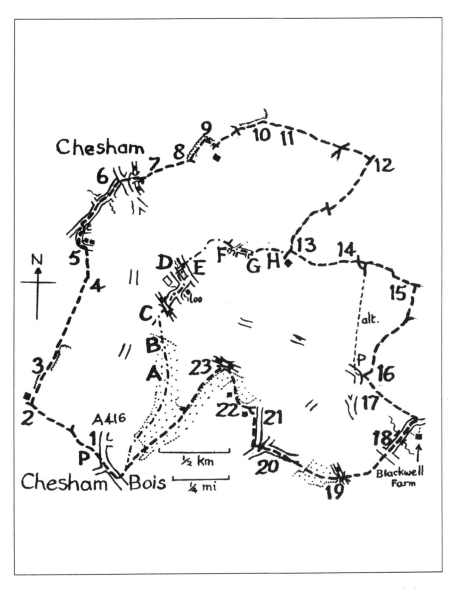

22. At footpath sign, go on (passing Warren Cottage on your L) and down path. Down steps and ½L for 50m.

23. L along track. R along main road.

Variations

North East from Chesham Bois (5 miles, 8km, 700ft): Go 150m along the A416 away from Chesham and 100m down track. Here fork L along path.

A. When fence on your L ends, go on along main path. At fork go on down to wood edge.

B. Go ½L down field.

C. ½R down track. On under railway and along road. Turn L just after passing tennis courts.

D. Turn R at end of row of houses and over river to main road.

E. Here L 20m, then R up Trapps Lane. It narrows later to a surfaced path.

F. When path ends, go on along Larks Rise to gate.

G. Here go L along field edge (hedge on your L) to corner stile.

H. Here L along track 20m, then R over stile and field to second stile. On down fields. Now follow 14 to 23.

Through Chesham (5½ miles, 8.5km, 600ft): Follow 1 to 12, then just before farm, turn R along field edge (hedge on your R) and down to kissing gate. Through gate and along road.

F. At sign 'Pheasant Rise', go on along surfaced path (houses on your L). At sign 'Whichcote Gardens', go ½L down track to main road.

E. On over road and bridge.

D. L along road, then R at T-junction. On up Hodds Wood Road and on under railway.

C. 100m further on, at stile, go ½L up field to wood.

B. Here keep on up into wood.

A. At top, keep by fence on your R. Go up track and R along road.

39. Chesham Ridges: A Short Stroll

Starting Point: Little Hundridge Lane (923 013).

Access: Leave Chesham on the B485 (Great Missenden) road. After going up the hill, turn R and park in the lane.

Distance: 3½ miles (5.5km).

Detail: A simple, horseshoe walk up one ridge and down another. You climb 250ft.

Map: Explorer 2 or Pathfinder 165.

There are at least ten attractive ridges radiating from Chesham, many of which are seen in walks 38 to 41. You pass Hundridge Manor (dating from the 18th century), and nearby a 13th-century chapel.

Spurs off the Bellingdon ridge, with Hawridge far right, seen from Chesham Vale
(see walk 41)

1. Carry on (N) along the lane. After dip go R to stile and on between fences.

2. On through gate with hedge, then wood, on your L.

3. Through small gate, R up field, then L along top of field. On over stile at field corner. On along tops of fields (hedge on your R).

4. At corner, go R then L along field edge to wood corner. (Or use track to same corner.)

5. On down track, then road.

6. Sharp R over stile just before house on R. Up through hedge gap, then L by hedge, then by wood.

7. Go on along track.

8. Through farm to field. Here R along track until past last cottage, and $\frac{2}{3}$L over stile to far field corner.

9. Over stile and on along road. Go R along lane.

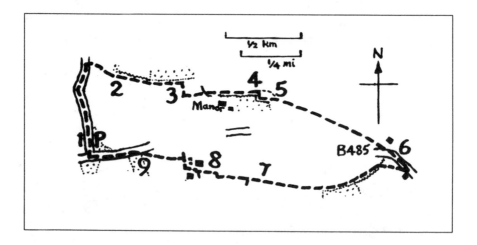

40. Chesham Ridges: A Longer Loop

Starting Point: Chartridge (929 038).

Access: Go NW from Chesham to Chartridge and park in Cogdells Lane, a left turn 300m past The Bell.

Distance: 7 miles (11.5km).

Detail: Plenty of ridges and ever-changing views. You climb 800ft.

Map: Explorer 2 or Pathfinder 165.

This switchback of a walk in open country also passes through the beeches of the delightful Captain's Wood. This has probably been there since the earliest settlement in the area in Saxon times, and the

Looking from Chartridge to Asheridge

hedge along its lower edge is also very old. Pednor House Farm is 15th century, with attractive dovecote and barns. For a pleasant 3½-mile two-ridge walk that also passes through this farm, park near point 17, follow 17 to 19 and return R down the lane.

1. Go R (SE) 170m along main road.

2. Turn L just before chapel. At field go on down its edge, soon between hedges. (If overgrown, use field edge L of hedges.)

3. Down field by hedge on your R. Up field towards L of several houses seen through wide gap in trees. Near top, go on by hedge on your L.

4. Turn R along road, then L into farm. Soon ½R for 20m, then ½L.

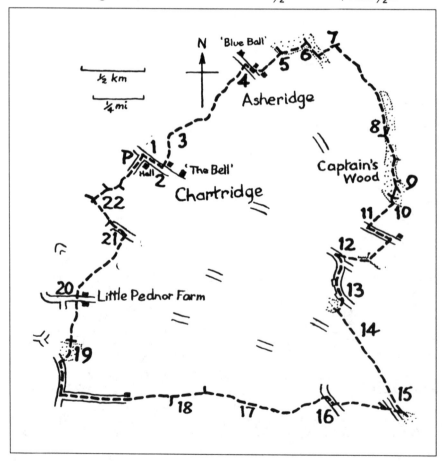

5. On down track in wood and R along its bottom.

6. At arrow go L through gap then ½R, soon ½L to top of field.

7. Here go R. For some time path follows top edge of fields.

8. On into wood, gently up track. Ignore minor paths off it. Soon after stile on L, you are at the top wood edge.

9. By next stile on L, track bears away from edge. Soon, at arrow, fork R along path. On over track.

10. Here path bears L to lower wood edge. Now go ½R down path.

11. L along road. Just before farm, go R over stile and up field. Keep R of fence. At top go under metal rail and between fences to drive and road.

12. Go L along road and R at fork.

13. R down track at end of second lay-by. Soon on down where track goes R. Path soon bears L.

14. On along top edge of field to gate, and on to stile.

15. Here sharp R down to wooden gate at road. Over road into field. Take the L of two paths, aiming towards valley. Over stile into next field. Bear slightly L to stile at road.

16. Go R along road. Soon L up track.

17. When clear path is seen between holly hedges, take this (beside track).

18. On along track, then lane. Go R at T-junction. At pine wood, fork R down path.

19. Go up field, over stile and ½R to stile. Here along path to lane.

20. On over lane to field corner. Here ½R over next field to its corner. Here over stile and down fields (hedge on your L).

21. Turn L along lane. Soon on along track.

22. As track bears L, go R up field (hedge on your R) to stile. On up track, then road.

Wayside and woodland flowers

Go to the woods early in the year, before the canopy of leaves has shut out the sunlight, and you will often find a delightful array of wild flowers, starting with wood anemonies in March, followed by wood sorrell, yellow archangel and of course sheets of bluebells. One speciality of the Chilterns is coralroot or coralwort, a plant with pinkish flowers resembling lady's smock, in flower in April. It is quite abundant in some beechwoods e.g. in the Hughenden valley and near Amersham. Another unique area is the small wood of box trees near Ellesborough (walk 29). Local place names like Boxmoor and Bix suggest it once occured more frequently. Mistletoe is sometimes seen high in the trees in the open e.g. near Stonor House (walk 7,8). The ghost orchid and red helleborine are two very rare orchids, the sites of which are not publicised.

Along your way, in hedges and banks, many other flowers may be seen: snowdrops, daffodils (escaped from gardens or planted by roadsides), violets and, though not in large quantities, primroses. Attractive trees include: the snow-white sloe, cherry and plum; whitebeam with its leaves which are densely furry-white underneath; spindle-tree with its lovely deep pinkish fruits which eventually open to reveal bright orange seeds. Scrambling over the hedges will be sweet-scented honeysuckle and old man's beard with its ultra-hairy seeds. Wild roses, white or pink, enhance the scene in June. Later in the year notewothy flowers are the foxgloves, greater knapweed (on which the marbled white butterfly is often seen) and nettle-leaved bellflower.

One final speciality is dragon's teeth (Tetragonolobus maritimus), a member of the pea family with pale yellow flowers which has made itself at home near Fingest (walk 6). It is in flower for several months in the summer.

41. Chartridge, Asheridge and Hawridge

Starting Point: Chartridge (929 038).

Access: Go NW from Chesham to Chartridge and park in Cogdells Lane, a left turn 300m past The Bell.

Distance: 7 miles (11.5km). Can be shortened.

Detail: Another chance to enjoy ridges and their views. You climb 900ft.

Map: Explorer 2 or Pathfinder 165.

A walk in the same area as walk 40, yet barely a mile of paths is common to both walks. (See that walk for the note on Captain's Wood.)

Entering Captain's Wood

1. Go R (SE) 170m along main road.

2. Turn L just before chapel. At field go on down its edge, soon between hedges. (If overgrown, use field edge L of hedges.)

3. Down field by hedge on your R. Up field towards L of several houses seen through wide gap in trees. Near top, go on by hedge on your L.

4. L along road. R between hedges just after the Blue Ball. Soon over field by hedge on your R.

5. Go up field (hedge on your R).

6. At top corner, go R over field and ½L over next field.

7. At field corner, go ½L to road, and R along it. Go past L turning (Bloomfield Cottages).

8. Go L along next drive. On to field and R along its edge to corner.

9. Here go sharp L, passing jutting out field corner to reach hedge gap.

10. Here go ½R down field (fence on your L) and over bottom stiles.

11. Go L to corner and R up field (hedge on your L).

12. Over stile 20m R of corner and up to ridge crest (hedge on your R).

13. Here R over stile and along crest.

14. At ridge path end, go L 100m then R by hedge (both on your L).

15. Go L over stile at corner.

16. R along road. L at signpost and through buildings until house is seen on your L.

17. Go R along the hedge which starts opposite the house.

18. On in wood 60m, and R down path. Bear L up wider path.

19. By a pit on your L (100m before end of wood), take R fork. At fence, go ½R to follow it down to wood corner.

20. Down to road (hedge on your L). Here R, soon L along drive and on up path.

21. Go R along road 50m, then L along road 100m.

22. Over road into wood. Soon bear R, then fork R to field. Follow wood edge to far L field corner.

23. Here L into wood and R along main path near top edge of wood. Path then goes gently down to bottom edge. ↘

24. Leave wood and turn L along by hedge, down and up.

25. R along road. Just after farm, go L down field with hedge on your L, but later on your R.

26. At bottom, on between hedges (or on path just R of hedge). On along drive.

27. Turn R along road.

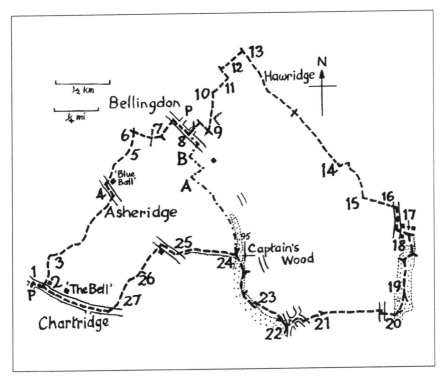

Variation

Shorter walk (5 miles, 8km, 500ft): Go N from Chesham to Bellingdon and turn R to park in side road (Bloomfield Cottages, 994 051). Walk along main road towards Chesham and follow 8-23. Then keep on just outside bottom edge of wood.(Use field if path is overgrown.)

A. At big holly tree at field corner, turn R between hedge and fence. Go L over stile 100m before house and along field edge to corner.

B. Here over stile and R to road. Then L along road to start.

42. Wendover Woods

Starting Point: Top of Aston Hill (891 102).

Access: On the A41, 1 mile W of Tring, turn SW on the A4011. Soon after a R turn, go L uphill to car park on L at top.

Distance: 6 miles (9.5km).

Detail: Several attractive woods, with the enclosed sections relieved by some open stretches and good views. You climb 900ft.

Map: Explorer 2 or Pathfinder 165.

You start at the hill where, in 1914, Lionel Martin drove up in a sports car from which the famous Aston Martin developed. Nearby Wendover is worth a visit for its 14th-century church and 16th-century buildings.

1. Go E along track on same side of road as car park.

2. Go ⅓L along path at gate by house. Later go R along road.

3. At road junction, go down field to hedge T-junction by pole. Go through hedge, L 5m, then R (beside hedge on your R).

4. At path T-junction in field corner, go L between hedges to bottom.

5. Here go on up over a crossing path. Soon bear R to climb in wood.

6. At road go L 50m, R over stile and across field. Look for large gap with pines each end. Aim for stile at the L side of gap.

7. Here on by wood on your L. On over road and along track.

8. Just before sunken track descends, climb the R bank. Go on down bank in wood. Later, path gently bears away from track below.

9. At bottom of dip, ignore paths on up and R up. Turn L down to track.

10. Here go L up track, soon on parallel path close by fence (on your R). Soon R along path (at first along wood edge).

11. Turn R down path. On down field, soon along its far edge.

12. Turn R over stile near houses and L down path. On along lane.

13. Turn R along track with field on your L. Soon ⅓L up path, later rejoining main track. (For views use edge paths L of track.)

14. Through gate at top, R on gravel track and at once ½L along track.

15. Go on gently up at fork.

16. Go ½R up steps. Later go on over drive. 50m later ignore small path forking R, but a further 50m on, fork R up next small path.

17. On over track to stile. Here ½L over field to far corner and L along road.

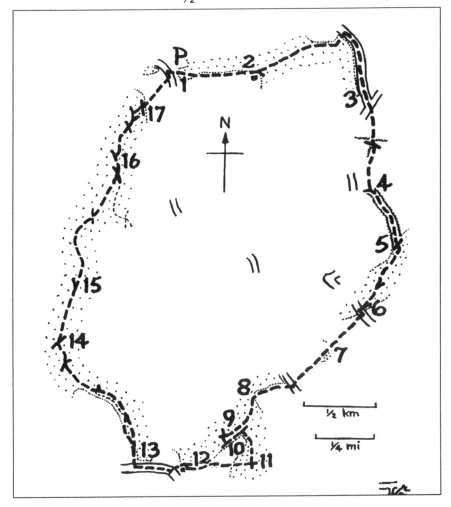

43. Near Tring

Starting Point: Just S of Tring (924 104).

Access: On the B4635, go W to the edge of Tring. Go on at roundabout, L at crossroads, R at T-junction then at once L. Park near bridge or at a R bend 300m beyond.

Distance: 6 miles (9.5km). Can be shortened.

Detail: An easy walk near the NE edge of the main Chiltern area. You climb 750ft.

Map: Explorer 2 or Pathfinder 165.

Pleasant woodland, rural views and a fine, final ridge that is little spoilt by the bypass. In Tring, the Natural History Museum (passed on the way to the parking) is attractive. It specialises in birds, butterflies, moths and mammals. The impressive 15th-century church has monuments, rood-screen, etc. In the woods, muddy patches can usually be bypassed.

1. Go up the lane, fork L, and at once fork R along track.
2. 50m before top of wood, go ½R along small path. On over field by fence on your R.
3. Where fence turns R, go ½L, soon by fence on your L. Go R along lane. On at junction.
4. When road turns R, go on in wood, never far from its L edge.
5. Over road and ½R along path by wood edge.
6. On over field (hedge on your L) and through two gates.
7. Go R along road 70m, then R over stile and across field to stile at wood corner. On beside wood edge to stile 80m before field corner.
8. L over stile, along path in wood. Keep on over track, path and track.
9. On over field (fence on your R), on to corner and on over lane.
10. Soon L along field edge. At field corner, L 10m and R up field.
11. R along lane (at T-junction). R at next lane T-junction.
12. Where lane turns R, go L up field.
13. Through hedge gap, L 5m, and R along track. Go ½R at junction.

14. Into wood and R along edge. Stay on rising track and ignore path forking R along edge.

15. Go L up track at next fork. Later pass R of house. ↷

16. Soon sharp L along track. At once, R along path (fence on your R).

17. Go L along lane. When it bears R, go on past barn and bear L along field edge, with wood on your L.

18. On when wood ends. At hedges, go on with hedge on your R.

19. At field corner, go ½R along by fence (parallel to road).

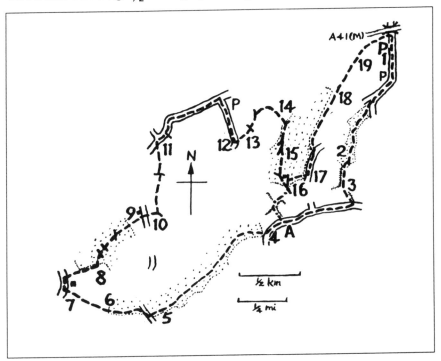

Variation

Shorter walk (4 miles, 6.5km, 500ft): From the above parking, drive on up lane, fork R, go R at T-junction and park at sharp L bend (914 092). Follow 4 to 15.

16. 80m before house on your R, go R through gate and over field to hedge gap. Here go through, ½L 30m, and ½L by hedge on your L.

A. Turn R along lane.

44. From Ashley Green

Starting Point: Ashley Green (977 052).

Access: From Berkhamstead on the A416, go L at the crossroads in Ashley Green for 100m and park on the L by the green.

Distance: 4½ miles (7km).

Detail: An easy, pleasant walk in an area seldom visited. You climb 450ft.

Map: Explorer 2 or Pathfinder 165.

Largely an open walk, with good views while you go down and up three times. If you carry on driving past the parking spot and turn L twice, you reach Grove Farm (987 043) after 2 miles. It is a 15th-century, fortified, domestic manor house with earthworks, remains of two gatehouses etc. It is the only one in the Home Counties.

The view of stage 3, rising to a farm

1. Walk N (towards Berkhamstead) along the green, with its edge not far to your R. Cross drive and go R along track at signpost. Soon fork R to gate then on between fences.

2. Soon ½L over stile and up field. Pass just L of trees. Over corner stiles and on to cross stile 200m along fence on your R.

3. Go down to R end of wood. Up by wood edge. After farm, go L up lane.

4. Go ½R to farm and on (buildings on your R).

5. Over stile and L by fence. On to cross stile and go R along track.

6. Turn R down lane, then track. At bottom, go R along path.

7. At top of rise, go R along track. R along lane. At U-turn, go L along track.

8. At L bend, go ½R down field to far end of trees and on to cross bottom stile.

9. Up path past pylon. Go ½L at path junction, now a hedge on your R.

10. At next path junction keep on, back to start.

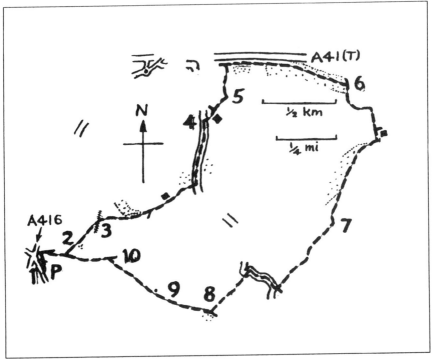

45. Gadding from Gaddesden

Starting Point: Great Gaddesden (029 113).

Access: Take the A4146 N from Hemel Hempstead, turn L to the village and park near the inn.

Distance: 5½ miles (8.5km).

Detail: An enjoyable variety of views of the Hertfordshire Chilterns. You climb 750ft.

Map: Pathfinder 166.

The River Gade is crossed for great views of its valley. Water End has some 17th-century cottages. Several ridges are then crossed, giving still more views. The 14th-century church at the end has Roman bricks and tiles in its walls. It may be muddy in stage 11.

1.   Go back to the A4146 and ⅓R along bottom of shallow valley.

2.   On over stile, now with fence on your R.

3.   Just after a crossing track, go R over stile, still with fence on your R. After 80m, go ½R through iron gate and on over stiles.

4.   Reach road just L of the L of two solitary houses. Here go R 10m and L between buildings and over stiles. Bear R to cross bridge and go on to field corner.

5.   Here go ½L over stile and up by hedge (on your R).

6.   At wood, go on up path near R edge.

7.   Near end of wood, fork L down to stile. On to road and over it.

8.   Go on 200m, then L to hedge corner. Here turn R, keeping hedge on your L. Keep on in next field, by fence.

9.   Go L into wood at stile, on by fence (on your L) and R along road.

10. Turn R down Browns Spring (at shops).

11. On along path when road goes R. Soon turn R along track.

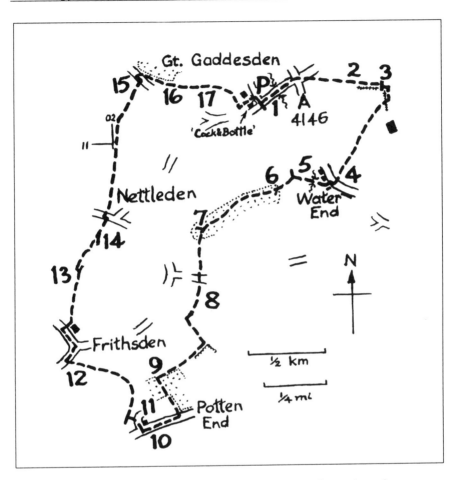

12. R at road, soon fork L. Just after Alford Arms go R up steep lane.

13. At top, go over stile and along field edge parallel to lane.

14. On down lane, L 20m at road and R by hedge (on your R) up to road.

15. Here go L 50m, over stile on your R, and along wood edge.

16. At end of wood, go over stile and field to double poles by hedge.

17. Here go through gap and $\frac{1}{2}$R down field to L end of wall under trees. Go $\frac{1}{2}$R along by wall and L over stile.

The infant River Gade near Waterend

46. North from Aldbury

Starting Point: Aldbury (965 125).

Access: Go NW from Berkhamstead on the A4251, R on the B4506 and L through Aldbury to the car park on L, 300m past the pond.

Distance: $3\frac{1}{2}$ miles (5.5km).

Detail: A splendid figure of eight from a delightful village. You climb 500ft.

Map: Explorer 2 or Pathfinder 165.

Along the first flat section, the wide view steadily improves. It is further enhanced as you climb a fine track in the second loop of the eight. Pleasant woods are met on the return. In the village are the often photographed old stocks beside the pond and the 16th-century manor house, with the Greyhound Inn beyond. Nearby is a mainly

The manor house, stocks and pond at Aldbury

13th- to 14th-century church. High above in the woods is the tall monument commemorating the canal-building Duke of Bridgewater. There may be mud in stages 9 and 10, avoided by returning along your outward route.

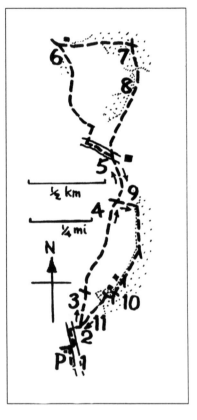

1. Walk to the far end of the car park, passing just R of building. Then R 5m and L along road. Soon R over stile.

2. Go L over stile and field to stile just L of brick wall.

3. On over drive and field with fence on your R (later on your L).

4. On over track and field. Go $\frac{1}{2}$L in next field.

5. Turn L along drive, R up path. At gate, go L up grass track.

6. Near house, go sharp R along track.

7. In wood, go R down path where track comes in on L. Leave wood and walk by another wood on your R.

8. On down field, and over drive, then $\frac{1}{2}$L over field.

9. Turn L up track. When it levels, fork R.

10. After house on R, go on over track and soon $\frac{1}{2}$R down path. Near house on R, fork L (signed 'Aldbury').

11. Over field to climb stile well L of far corner. Now $\frac{1}{2}$R to road and L along it.

47. Ivinghoe Hills

Starting Point: Pitstone Hill car park (954 149).

Access: From Ivinghoe, go S on the B488. Soon go straight on when the road turns R. Park at the hilltop.

Distance: 7½ miles (12km). Easily shortened.

Detail: A beautiful ridge walk with plenty of views. You climb 900ft.

Map: Explorer 2 or Pathfinder 165.

This is unique – a 4-mile ridge with eight summits, all but one of which can be visited, though one or two need a minor detour. The ridge is divided into two parts near the car park. The approach to the N half closely encounters the spectacular Incombe Hole, a combe which is 250ft deep. The Beacon has traces of one of the oldest Iron

Ivinghoe Beacon

Age forts in England (700BC) and two tumuli. This is the end of the long-distance Ridgeway path and has extensive views. Pitstone Hill, in the S half, has many signs of ancient habitation, including Grim's Ditch and some holes and mounds which are the remains of the shafts and waste tips of Neolithic flint mines (950 148). Aldbury Nowers is a lovely beech-covered hill.

1. At car park, cross road and go on over field. ↘
2. Go on past signpost. The track bears L. Leave it at gate and stile. Go on along path in the open, then through wood.
3. Down field 150m to stile. Here go ½R up path and later down.
4. Over road and ½L up gently rising path. At Beacon turn R.
5. At both crossing fences, keep on down ridge. Then R down track.
6. At bottom hedge go R along track.
7. Go through gate and bear L. 50m before next gate, go R up track (it soon becomes clear).
8. Turn L along road. Soon go R along track.
9. Fork ½R down track when your track is seen bending R ahead. Soon go on down when larger track is met.
10. Keep on through farm. Turn L along road.
11. R over stile and along by hedge. As hedge turns L, go on over field.
12. On over track, towards and over distant stile. ↘
13. L beside fence. As it turns ⅔L, join sunken path, which bears L to stile.
14. Go over stile and along path which enters wood.
15. After steps, go R down track at 4-way sign. After 10m fork R along path.
16. Go ½R along drive. Near buildings go L over two stiles and on.
17. On over the R-hand of two stiles and R up path. Over stile and ½L along path, with quarry fence on your L. (Later, for better views, use small path gently rising away from fence.)
18. Follow sunken track bearing R to ridge top. Here go L along ridge.

Variations

To Aldbury Nowers (5 miles, 7.5km, 500ft): Follow 1, then go R at signpost (hedge on your R). Over stile and on up path. At junction go R down track. Follow 10 to 18.

To Ivinghoe Beacon (6 miles, 9.5km, 650ft): Follow 1 to 12, then turn R along ridge.

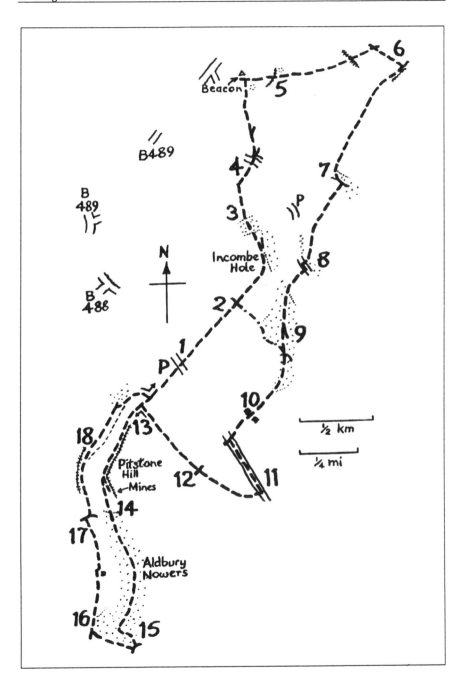

48. From Ivinghoe Village

Starting Point: Ivinghoe (945 163).

Access: From Dunstable, go SW on the B489. Go R along the B488 into Ivinghoe, forking R just before the church. Soon fork R again and park in Wellcroft.

Distance: 4½miles (7km).

Detail: An easy, open walk with the option of reaching Ivinghoe Beacon. You climb 500ft.

Map: Explorer 2 or Pathfinder 165.

You follow the ancient Icknield Way, but leave it to approach the Beacon. There you follow a fine, high, level route before returning. You can detour to see Pitstone Mill, one of England's oldest post windmills. The National Trust open it on bank holiday and summer Sunday afternoons. The tall church (13th to 15th century) has much of interest: 'poppyhead' carvings on medieval bench ends showing strange, pagan 'green men'; fine 'stiff-leaf' carving on the capitals of the nave arches; and carved angels in the Perpendicular roof. Outside, the 18ft hook hanging on a wall was used to pull thatch off burning roofs. Nearby are a small, Tudor manor house, 16th-century Old Vicarage and Victoria Cottage. Through the yard of Ford End Farm (941 166), by the road to Linslade), there is a restored watermill that is occasionally open and working. There was a mill there in the 14th century, but this one may be later.

1. Carry on along Wellcroft and on along path.

2. Just before reaching road, go ½R to small gate and up field edge.

3. Go R at field corner then 20m to gate, L through it and R beside hedge.

4. Near field corner, go L beside fence. On through gate to road.

5. Go R along road and L up minor road 100m. At sign go L up path.

6. After 30m, go R along small path parallel to road. (Don't go up to the clearer path close to the shrubby area.) The path becomes clearer and climbs to pass just L of a small hill.

7. At road, go on up track opposite. Soon fork R along path on the side of ridge.

8. At gate, go on along nearly level path. Later, it gently climbs and bears L past trough, keeping clear of wood on your L.

9. On towards gate and stile, but before reaching them, bear R on clear path with steep valley on your R. On down track that bears R.

10. As track nears stile, go R along by fence to another stile. L over this and ⅔R down field.

11. The path bears L and soon R in next field to reach L end of a line of trees. Keep on to road. (Go L along road, then path, to visit windmill.)

12. Go R along road back to village.

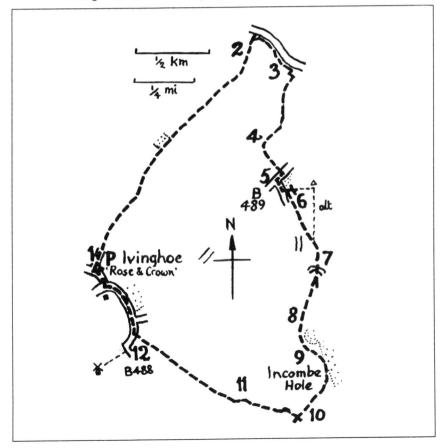

Ivinghoe village and its windmill

49. Dunstable Downs

Starting Point: Downs car park (008 197).

Access: Go SW from Dunstable on the B489. At the outskirts, go L along the B4541 and park at the top.

Distance: 4$\frac{1}{2}$ miles (6.5km). Easily halved.

Detail: A fine, open walk with plenty of views. You climb 500ft.

Map: Pathfinder 165 and 166.

This is where the Chilterns end, although further NE there are a few small hills. The 'Five Knolls' are Neolithic and Bronze Age burial mounds. Skeletons of Saxon warriors were found in them. In medieval times there was a gallows here. It is a popular walking and gliding area. At the S end you may spot the Whipsnade chalk lion and other foreign animals.

Dunstable Downs with hang-gliders

1. Go N (towards Dunstable) along top of the downs, soon by fence on your L until you go through gate.

2. When you descend, go on to smooth, green field. There go L 20m, and L again along shady path. Through gate and along main path. It soon goes down and along by field edge.

3. There are three dips. Ignore the second (and its crossing path). At the third, go ½L up clear path. Soon fork L to keep dense shrubs on your R. Later cross over track.

4. Bear ½R at open downland. Make for the L (top) end of shrubby area. Here, go ½R along path, with fence on your L.

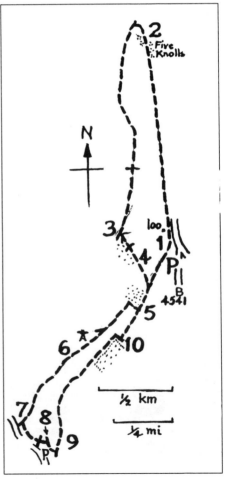

5. Just before gate, go R 100m, and L along field edge, passing by two pylons. (Ignore path going ½R before pylons are reached).

6. On down R bank of sunken track.

7. Over stile 15m before road and L up path. On over sunken path.

8. Soon ½R along path to car park. Up steps and L 100m along field edge.

9. Through gate and on along level path by field edge (hedge on your R).

10. At far corner of wood (on your R), go R and soon L to far corner of field. Go through gate and on to start.

50. North of Whipsnade

Starting Point: Downs car park (008 197).

Access: Go SW from Dunstable on the B489. At the outskirts, go L along the B4541 and park at the top.

Distance: 4 miles (6km).

Detail: Easy walking from the downs to Whipsnade. You climb 300ft.

Map: Pathfinder 166.

After the views from the downs you pass the zoo and a Tree Cathedral, with trees planted to represent features of a church. Services are sometimes held there. More views in farmland on the way back. There may be some mud on the track in stage 2.

The view near Green End Farm

1. Go SW (away from Dunstable) along top of the downs, with gentle slope on R and many low posts 30m to the L.
2. On along edge of small wood, with fence on your L. On out of wood. L along track at field corner.
3. On over drive. Soon fork R into wood. On along drive.
4. R along path at sign 'Whipsnade', and soon L just before gate into the Tree Cathedral. Bear L to road and L along it.
5. Just after crossroads, go ½L up path in wood.
6. On leaving wood, go either side of hedge. (If on R of hedge, go through gap near field corner.) On over open field past tree.
7. Turn R along lane. Soon L over stile and down track. At gate go ½R down field and ½R along same track as before.
8. At barn, go on to bottom by hedge on your L. Then ½L up to stile and along nearly level path.
9. Over stile and down into wood. Go L along track in field.
10. As track goes L, you go R and at once L along field edge (hedge on your L).
11. At top, go ½L through trees and on to lane. Go R along lane.

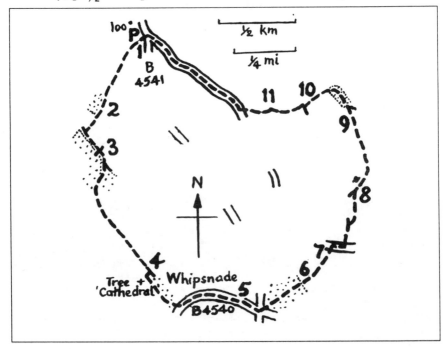

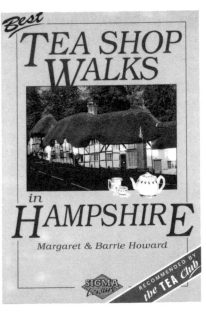

Also of interest:

Best Tea Shop Walks in The Chilterns

Best Tea Shop Walks in Surrey & Sussex

Best Tea Shop Walks in Hampshire

Best Tea Shop Walks in Suffolk

(Note: Many more areas are covered in our 'Best Tea Shop Walks' series; each book is £6.95)

By-Way Biking in The Chilterns (£6.95)

Best Pub Walks in & around Central London (£6.95)

Best Pub Walks in Essex (£6.95)

Dogs' London: The City's Best Walks for Dogs and their Owners (£6.95)

London Bus-Top Tourist (£6.95)

Railway Rambles: London & The South-East (£5.95)

Walks in Mysterious Hampshire (£6.95)

A Year of Walks: Sussex (£6.95)

West Sussex Church Walks (£6.95)